# Seven Wonders

# Seven Wonders

### Everyday Things
### for a Healthier Planet

## John C. Ryan

SIERRA CLUB BOOKS
San Francisco

The Sierra Club, founded in 1892 by John Muir, has devoted itself to the study and protection of the Earth's scenic and ecological resources—mountains, wetlands, woodlands, wild shores and rivers, deserts and plains. The publishing program of the Sierra Club offers books to the public as a nonprofit educational service in the hope that they may enlarge the public's understanding of the Club's basic concerns. The point of view expressed in each book, however, does not necessarily represent that of the Club. The Sierra Club has some sixty chapters coast to coast, in Canada, Hawaii, and Alaska. For information about how you may participate in its programs to preserve wilderness and the quality of life, please address inquiries to Sierra Club, 85 Second Street, San Francisco, CA 94105.

www.sierraclub.org/books

Copyright © 1999 by Northwest Environment Watch

www.northwestwatch.org

Published by Sierra Club Books, in conjunction with Random House, Inc.

Library of Congress Cataloging-in-Publication Data
Ryan, John C.
Seven wonders: everyday things for a healthier planet/John C. Ryan.
p.      cm.
Includes bibliographical references.
ISBN 1-57805-038-3
1. Ecological engineering.   I. Title.
GE350.R9   1999        628—dc21          99-22858

Printed in the United States of America on 100 percent recycled paper

2   4   6   8   9   7   5   3   1

# Acknowledgments

One person's name appears on the cover of this book, but it took a cast of dozens to bring the book into the world. I wrote *Seven Wonders* for Northwest Environment Watch (NEW), an independent nonprofit research center based in Seattle, and I owe an especially large debt to Ken Baldwin, Erik Haunreiter, and Marla Pallin, the three research interns who volunteered hundreds of hours to research NEW's tenth book with me. Their work shows on every page.

My greatest intellectual debt is to NEW's executive director Alan Durning. *Seven Wonders* grew out of "The Seven Sustainable Wonders of the World," an article Alan wrote for the March/April 1994 *Utne Reader.* I am also grateful for ideas and criticisms shared by *Seven Wonders'* reviewers: Andy Clarke, Rick Heede, Judy Jacobsen, Nick Lenssen, David Pimentel, Isabel Stirling, and Mathis Wackernagel, as well as most of the staff at NEW. Of course, any errors or just plain dumb ideas remaining in the book are my fault and no one else's.

Everyone affiliated with Northwest Environment Watch helped in their own way to get this book into your hands, and I thank them: editorial director Ellen Chu, office manager and volunteer coordinator Rhea Connors, executive director Alan Durning, former communications director Lizzie Grossman, membership assistants

Yoram Bauman and Meg O'Leary, and membership director Steve Sullivan. The staff of NEW's sister organization in Canada, NEW BC, includes executive director Donna Morton and office manager Amanda Pawlowski.

Much, if not most, of NEW's work is performed by dedicated volunteers, including interns Russel Buri, Nicholas Dankers, Sarah Howard, Judith Kmileck, Joanna Lemly, Meg O'Leary, Owen Reynolds, Leila Sievanen, Erika Swahn, and Jennifer Tice. Our talented crew of volunteers also includes Mark Gibbs, Lynn Gordon, Russell Jones, Dana Klein, Norman Kunkel, Lyn McCollum, Ajitha Rao, John Wedgwood, Darrel Weiss, and Suzy Whitehead. Northwest Environment Watch is guided by its all-volunteer board of directors: John Atcheson, Mae Burrows, Sandi Chamberlain, Aaron Contorer, Alan Durning, Jeff Hallberg, Sandra Hernshaw, and David Yaden.

Financial support for this book was provided by approximately fifteen hundred individual contributors to NEW as well as the Brainerd Foundation, Bullitt Foundation, C. S. Fund, Nathan Cummings Foundation, William and Flora Hewlett Foundation, Horizons Foundation, Henry P. Kendall Foundation, Lazar Foundation, Merck Family Fund, True North Foundation, Turner Foundation, and Weeden Foundation.

*Seven Wonders* was ably edited, in tag-team fashion, by Ellen Chu at NEW, Danny Moses at Sierra Club Books, and Beth Gibson at Random House.

I'd like to thank my grandmother Virginia Rykoskey and my mother, Nancy Neal, for the genes and everything else, and my friend Lana Kuxhausen for her support throughout the research and writing of this book.

Finally, I'm grateful to my activist friends in Indonesia—Chairil, Iis, Lili, Monty, Pilin, Priyana, Sandra, Yance, and Yoga, among others—for showing me what it is to live both simply and audaciously.

# Contents

# Seven Wonders

# Prologue:
# The Dalai Lama
# vs. *Baywatch*

When the Dalai Lama, spiritual leader of Tibet, met with economist John Kenneth Galbraith, he asked the Harvard professor a simple but penetrating question: "What would the world be like if everyone drove a motor car?" The Tibetan cleric probably did not intend it, but his question constitutes a koan: a paradoxical riddle of Zen Buddhist tradition. A koan has no logical answer—"What is the sound of one hand clapping?"—but the search for a solution may lead to a flash of enlightenment.

The Dalai Lama's question is a koan because its answer depends on an impossibility. If all the world drove as we do in North America—the only continent with nearly as many motor vehicles as people of driving age—global petroleum consumption would quadruple. Yet oil production will never quadruple: many petroleum geologists predict that world oil production is nearing its peak and will begin a permanent decline within 10 to 25 years. A planet of North American–style drivers would cause the world's emissions of heat-trapping carbon dioxide to double, even as climatologists agree that we need to cut back by 60 percent or more worldwide to stabilize our climate.

Long before everyone could step on the gas, traffic jams, fatal collisions, and smog would reach catastrophic levels. Even if the vast majority of the world's people could afford to own a car (they cannot), most governments would be bankrupted trying to build the necessary highways, parking lots, and emergency rooms. Production of basic raw materials like iron, aluminum, and rubber—and the habitat loss and pollution caused by these industries—would all have to multiply several times.

Cars clearly fail the Dalai Lama test: could everyone in the world enjoy them? This doesn't mean that people shouldn't have cars, but it does mean that the North American way of life cannot be a model for the world. This fact, in turn, wouldn't be such a problem except for what you might call the *Baywatch* effect.

Each week, a billion people in 140 countries tune in to *Baywatch* (or *Soul of the Sea*, as it's known in China), the most watched series in television history. This swimsuit video disguised as drama is only one of the more scantily clad examples of America's biggest export—its culture. With so much of the world watching us on TV, most of the world wants to live like us (or at least like the wealthier, more photogenic versions of us on globally popular programs like *Dallas* and *Beverly Hills 90210*). For better or worse, people everywhere are chasing the American Dream of sport utility vehicles in the garage and steaks on the grill.

Yet nowhere else do humans place nearly as many demands on the Earth as we do in North America. In energy terms, a human's food consumption is similar to that of a common dolphin—about 2,500 to 3,000 calories per day. But with all the other energy we use (mostly from fossil fuels), the average North American consumes about 180,000 calories each day—about six times as much as the average human. It is also the daily appetite of a sperm whale. We consume so much more than one might expect for the midsized mammals that we are, "it's as if each of us were trailing a big Macy's-parade balloon around, feeding it constantly," in the words of author Bill McKibben.

The giant Bullwinkles and Spidermen bobbing behind us have left indelible marks on our world. Most notably, North America has led the world in emitting the greenhouse gases that have already started changing the entire planet's climate. We humans also use or degrade 40 percent of the vegetation that grows on land each year, as well as one third of the fresh water flowing through inhabited regions. We have degraded two thirds of the world's forests and three fourths of its grasslands, added at least 250 new chemicals to the body fat of virtually every human being, and unleashed the greatest mass extinction of species since dinosaurs roamed the Earth.

*Ouch.*

Just as one hand clapping cannot make a sound, a world of six billion North American–style consumers cannot come to pass. But pondering such a world can help us see our own in a different light. What *can* we and people everywhere safely use in our daily lives? The koan helps steer us toward new ways of addressing the basic challenge of living on a crowded planet—sustainability. How can people get the nutrition, shelter, knowledge, recreation, and community they need without placing insupportable demands on the world?

The flip side of our economy's current destructiveness is that opportunities abound to lessen our impacts on the Earth—and improve human welfare as well. When it comes to sustainability, North Americans are standing in the grandmother of all orchards with a bumper crop of low-hanging fruit. Our economy is so inefficient at using what it takes from the Earth that most of the appalling environmental damage we do can be avoided without hardship. In agriculture, industry, transportation, and all realms of daily life, workable alternatives—superior to and usually less expensive than business as usual—already exist. Knowing that our economy can work better and less harmfully than it does can give a much-needed sense of hope in the midst of disheartening ecological deterioration.

Hope *is* needed because there are big challenges ahead, and they can seem daunting. Stabilizing the world's climate while allowing the billion people living in absolute poverty a decent economic future will require industrial nations to reduce their emissions of carbon dioxide by at least 75 to 90 percent—to a fourth or a tenth of their current levels. Other global ecological problems require similarly sweeping reforms. This magnitude of change won't happen overnight. Yet these are the sorts of goals we need to aim for.

Fortunately, all the tools needed to slash our economy's impacts severalfold—to help us take quantum leaps, not plodding steps, toward sustainability—already exist. This book is about seven of them, the seven sustainable wonders of the world. Unlike the wonders of the ancient world, the seven sustainable wonders are notable not for grandeur or antiquity but for their ability to get jobs done at minimal cost to the Earth. They are wondrous because, unlike most artifacts of our modern economy, they pass the Dalai Lama test: everyone on Earth could use them without overtaxing the planet's finite natural wealth.

The items portrayed in this book can help us bring our sperm whale–sized appetites down to a human scale again, our gargantuan impacts down to a level the Earth can support. These seven are not the only, or even the most important, tools for sustainability. As with every "seven wonders" list since the Greek poet Antipater first made his more than 2,000 years ago, wonder is to some degree in the eye of the beholder. But all seven of these sustainable wonders are exceptionally powerful at improving human life at little or no cost to nature—arguably the central challenge of the twenty-first century. Like the Dalai Lama's koan, all seven can also help us see our lives in a new light and start to understand what it means to accept or reject the challenge to live more sustainably.

Remarkably, each item on this list predates the turn of the twentieth century; some even predate the Great Pyramid of Egypt, the only one of the seven wonders of the ancient world still standing. But this book is not a tirade against technology. Advanced technologies— such as fuel cells that are twice as effective as internal-combustion engines at squeezing energy out of a tank of gas—can help us take great strides toward sustainability. It's just that high tech is hyped by all sorts of businesses and government agencies; it doesn't need any extra help here.

Many simpler wonders, on the other hand, are in danger of being abandoned when they should be entering their golden age. Unlike the Great Pyramid—which remains great despite sitting almost unused for 3,000 years—the sustainable wonders depend on people making use of them. It will take concerted action, by individuals and by society, to help these ordinary things realize their wondrous potential.

This book is the latest in a long line of lists to heap praise on wonders of the ancient, historic, and modern worlds. The lists (always in sevens) consist mostly of colossal monuments to deities, leaders, or engineering skills (including the occasional bizarre item like the Chicago sewage disposal system). The seven sustainable

wonders, on the other hand, are not monuments to past achieve-
ments or technologies but tools to help us live. They look forward,
not backward; the only thing colossal about them is the ecological
harm they all fight. These unlikely objects—mostly small and
unimposing—can help us build a civilization that can last through
the ages, a feat that should leave us all filled with wonder.

# The Bicycle

I remember clearly the morning of April 2, 1997. I left the house by the back door, keys in hand, ready to slide onto the driver's seat and head down the driveway to work. But there was just an empty space where I had left my vehicle. I couldn't comprehend for a second: did I park somewhere else last night? Then it dawned on me: my traveling companion for nearly a decade, my 1987 Cannondale 18-speed bicycle, had been stolen.

It's silly to get so attached to a piece of aluminum and steel, but having my bicycle stolen from my own back porch felt almost like losing a limb. For nine years, that bike had been my almost daily companion, even part of my identity. Maybe my relationship with the Cannondale had become unhealthy, too close. I can see myself on an upcoming *Oprah*: "Men Who Love Their Vehicles Too Much." I could be a guest right next to a guy who buys spray-on dirt to make his sport ute look like he actually takes it off road.

North Americans might not believe it, but my love affair with my vehicle puts me, not my *Oprah* sofa-mate, squarely in the transportation mainstream. The bicycle is the world's most widely used transport vehicle. Worldwide, bicycles outnumber automobiles almost two to one, and their production outpaces cars' three to one. Rush-hour traffic in China is dominated by human-powered vehicles; even in the wealthy cities of Europe and Japan, large shares of the populace get around by bike.

Despite its popularity elsewhere, the bicycle gets little use or respect, except as a plaything, in North America. About 50 million American adults (and 40 million children) ride bikes at least once each year, but only about 2 million are regular bike commuters. Of all trips in the United States, just two thirds of 1 percent are made by bicycle. Similarly, only 1 percent of Canadian commuters report bicycling as their usual mode of transportation. Some government agencies have embraced bikes, but they remain the exception. More typical is Transport Canada's 1997 annual report on the nation's transportation system: in 210 pages, it doesn't even mention bicyclists, except as victims of traffic accidents.

The bicycle—the most energy-efficient form of travel ever devised—deserves better. Pound for pound, a person on a bicycle expends less energy than any creature or machine covering the same distance. (A human walking spends about three times as much energy per pound; even a salmon swimming spends about twice as much.)

I love riding a bike because of all it does for my wallet, my health, even my legs. But bicycles are sustainable wonders because of what they *don't* do to the world. A bicyclist's breathing (the closest a bike comes to exhaust) doesn't acidify the rain or kill people with carbon monoxide and particulates; neither does it alter the global climate. A bicyclist fuels up on carbohydrates, not fossil fuels and imported oil. Bicycles don't cause traffic jams or require paving over whole landscapes at the expense of croplands, government coffers, and livable neighborhoods. And bicycles are not the leading killer of Americans and Canadians 2 to 24 years old or, worldwide, of men 15 to 44 years old. That distinction is reserved for the automobile.

An amazing invention, the automobile has given twentieth-century humans unprecedented mobility. Yet cars have proliferated to the detriment of all other means of getting around and at great expense to human and natural communities. Today, Americans make 86 percent of all trips by car and drive their motor vehicles as many miles as all drivers in the rest of the world combined. "Two cars in the garage" no longer suffices as the American Dream: one in five American households now owns three vehicles or more. Cars so dominate transportation systems and communities in North America that their own usefulness is on the wane: they are crowding themselves to a standstill.

Though people worldwide aspire to the American Dream of cars in every garage, it is an impossible dream for the world as a whole. Even ignoring the ecological toll, the economic costs alone prohibit the dream's coming true. Fewer than 10 percent of humans can afford to buy a car (roughly 80 percent of humans can afford to buy a bicycle). Building the necessary roads and parking spaces would bankrupt governments and probably threaten world food supplies. China, for example, would have to pave the equivalent of 40 percent of the nation's cropland to give each of its citizens access to as much pavement as an American has.

Activists, engineers, and planners are working hard to promote alternatives to our problematic, car-dominated system. Buses, trains, and carpools produce less pollution and traffic than solo driving—but lack the privacy and door-to-door convenience of cars. Vehicles powered by alternative fuels or electricity, and proposed "hypercars" able to cross the continent on a tank of gas, could minimize cars' greenhouse gas emissions. But such cars do nothing about the problems of traffic, sprawl, or deadly accidents. Though a variety of choices is key to reforming our car-centered transportation system, the only vehicle that addresses all the environmental liabilities of cars is the bicycle.

Bicycles are not for everyone, and they're not for every trip. Cars do many things that bicycles cannot easily do: carry heavy loads uphill, protect riders from the elements, and cover long distances quickly. But a surprising number of car trips could easily be made by bike. Nearly half of all trips in the United States are three miles or less; more than a quarter are less than a mile. While advertising sells cars and trucks as tools for the open road, they most often help us inhabit a small daily realm—"Errandsville"—defined by home, store, job, and school. Many of these trips are easily bikable—or walkable—even on roads designed without bicycles or pedestrians in mind. A bicyclist can easily cover a mile in 4 minutes, a pedestrian in 15.

Many more of these short trips would be made under human power if bike-friendly amenities like bike lanes, paved shoulders, and shower facilities were common. Nearly half the recreational riders in the United States—or one out of five of all adults—say they would sometimes bike to work if better bike lanes or paths existed. Among major U.S. cities, those with extensive bicycle lanes have three times the rate of bike commuting as other cities.

Short car trips are, naturally, the easiest to replace with a bike (or even walking) trip. Mile for mile, they are also the most polluting. Engines running cold, at typical urban speeds, produce four times the carbon monoxide and twice the volatile organic compounds (VOCs) as engines running hot. And at the end of a trip, smog-forming (and carcinogenic) VOCs continue to evaporate from an engine until it cools off, whether the engine's been running for five minutes or five hours.

Fortunately for everyone who racks up frequent-biker miles, bikers (and pedestrians) are actually exposed to less air pollution than people in cars. Automobile exhaust tends to form an invisible tunnel along the roadway, and pollutants are most concentrated near the middle. Drivers near the tunnel's center pass through air two to three times more polluted than pedestrians and bikers at the tunnel's outer edge, who are exposed to roughly twice the background level of contaminants. Because cars offer little or no protection from pollutants, car riders bear the full brunt of car exhaust. Bus riders—sitting much higher off the ground—breathe somewhat less pollution, while bikers inhale the least.

Motor vehicles threaten bikers' health in a much less subtle manner, though: collisions. In surveys, bicyclists consistently point to traffic safety as the single greatest deterrent to bicycling for everyday transportation. Cruising down a road with nothing more than a helmet for protection does leave one feeling exposed to the tons of metal rushing past. In 1996, nearly 42,000 people were killed in motor vehicle crashes in the United States, of whom 5,412 were pedestrians and 761 were bicyclists. Ninety-six percent of the bicyclist victims were not wearing helmets. (The same year, 3,082 Canadians, including 59 bikers, were killed.) Lacking safe places to bike, bikers face a greater average risk of being killed by a car in each mile or trip than drivers do. (Motorcycles—which combine the speed of automobiles with the exposure of bicycles—are many times more likely to get their users killed.) On-street bike lanes and off-street bike paths would make bicycling far safer. Universal helmet use alone could prevent more than half of all bicycling fatalities.

Though riding the roads has its risks, bicycling's health benefits far outweigh them. As a form of exercise, bicycling—low-impact, aerobic, easy, and inexpensive—is hard to beat. (Despite the accident risk, bicycling is actually one of the safer forms of exercise: an hour on a bike is less likely to injure you than an hour of baseball or basketball.) Increased use of bicycles as transportation could help reduce the huge toll of sedentary lifestyles on North Americans. In the United States, more people are at risk of heart disease—the nation's leading killer—due to physical inactivity than any other factor, including smoking and fat-laden diets. Forty percent of all American adults get almost no exercise; only 1 out of 13 gets the recommended amount. Even light to moderate exercise—like walking or biking—can reduce the risk of diseases ranging from high blood pressure and osteoporosis to cancer. It might also reduce the traffic of people driving to health clubs to sit on exercise bikes.

To make biking as healthy as possible, I wear a helmet and assume that every parked car is a door-opener until proven otherwise. I also try to minimize my contact with inattentive cell phone cradlers by sticking to side roads or bike lanes whenever possible. But there is only so much any individual can do to reduce the risks. Government action is essential to provide safer and more appealing places to ride.

Policies from local zoning laws to federal highway funding and tax codes favor driving over all other modes of transport; revised policies can just as effectively do the reverse. In the California cities of Davis and Palo Alto, crisscrossed with bike lanes, at least one out of five trips is made by bicycle. In Japan, which has a similar rate of bicycle ownership but higher gasoline taxes and more restrictive parking than the United States, one out of six workers relies on bicycles for the daily commute. Bike-friendly policies, from traffic calming to carfree downtown zones, have boosted cycling rates in five European nations to 10 percent or more of urban trips; one fifth of all trips in Danish cities are made by bike, and one third in Dutch cities.

By slowing cars down, traffic-calming measures like street-narrowing curb bulbs and traffic diverters at intersections make streets safer and more pleasant for everyone—not just bikers. With traffic accidents the leading killer of North American children, traffic speed is the decisive factor in determining how safe a neighborhood is for children. A pedestrian hit by a car traveling at 40 miles per hour (65 kph) has a 15 percent chance of surviving; the same person has a 55 percent chance of surviving at 30 miles per hour (50 kph) and a 95 percent chance at 20 miles per hour (30 kph). Most North American youths come of age when they get their driver's licenses at age 16; by contrast, many Dutch children start traveling about town on their own at age 4, when they learn to bike. America's menacing streets deny children the freedom to explore their surroundings and reduce parents to modern centaurs: half human, half minivan.

Ours is a car culture, but it's easy to forget that one out of three people in both the United States and Canada cannot drive. Children, the elderly, the disabled, and those who cannot afford to drive are often stranded by our transportation system. More compact cities with safe and pleasant streetscapes benefit not only people who can choose their desired mode of transportation but also those for whom driving is not an option. A surprising number of non-drivers could be bikers, given half a chance: in Europe's compact and bikable cities, even many senior citizens bicycle, helping them maintain vitality and prolong active, independent lives. In large cities in China, 20 percent of people older than 60 bicycle as their primary mode of transportation.

Taxpayers and budget cutters are other constituencies that should support bicycling. Conditions for bicyclists can be improved cheaply and quickly: often it takes only a bucket of paint to make a bike lane or shave unneeded width off a car lane. Other programs— like building bike paths or installing bike racks—are more expensive but still cheaper than similar investments for cars because bikes take up so little space to use and park. It costs as much as 20 times more to support a passenger-mile of automobile traffic than one of bicycle traffic.

Bicycles are a far cheaper way of providing mobility for the masses, but in the end, it's not *mobility* that people really want; it's *access.* When destinations are closer together, people can do the things they want to do with less time and energy spent in transit. And compact urban form encourages alternative modes of travel: more trips are easily walkable or bikable, and mass transit becomes more cost-effective with more riders per area. In the long run, the measures most crucial to getting more people on their feet and on their bikes are those that fight sprawl and encourage dense, livable cities. On average, city dwellers drive a third less than—and half as fast as—suburbanites. To legalize and encourage the mixing of homes, shops, and offices, local zoning codes need to be revised. And tax codes and land-use regulations need to reward builders who fill in the underused space in existing cities and towns, not those who turn farms and forests into "Foxmeadow Farms" subdivisions and "Cedar Knolls" business parks.

Biking has made progress in North America in recent years. Many localities and a few states have begun to redesign their streets to better accommodate cyclists and pedestrians. Fifty-five North American cities have bike racks on their buses; individuals in at least 40 cities and towns in the United States and Canada have created "free ride" programs where specially marked bicycles are left out for anyone to use. And at least 1,200 police departments in the two nations have bicycle squads, lending further respectability to bikes as effective tools for mobility.

Perhaps the most important pro-bicycle milestone in North America in recent years was the passage of ISTEA (short for . . . never mind; just call it "ice tea" like everyone else) by the U.S. Congress in 1991. Under ISTEA, 1 percent of federal transportation funding has supported projects improving conditions for pedestrians and cyclists, including the creation of bike and pedestrian coordinator positions in every state and the funding of bike lanes, bike racks, and other facilities around the nation. It was reauthorized in 1998 only after a long struggle by advocates of alternative transportation. Yet this measure pales when compared with those in nations that make bicycling a priority: the Netherlands, for example, spends 10 percent of its roads budget to support bicycle facilities. For the moment, most city and suburban streets in North America remain inhospitable to anyone who is not in a car, and sprawl still rules the day. Imagine trying to walk or bike a mile in any direction from a shopping mall near your home. Then think instead about making your next shopping trip somewhere you *can* walk or bike home from.

A bicycle is radically different from a car in its simplicity, power source, and environmental impact: the idea that bikes can do many of the jobs that cars now do may take some getting used to. But thinking differently is the only way to do more than fiddle at the margins of the world's burning environmental problems. After all, we in the industrial world need to reduce our greenhouse gas emissions by some 90 percent to tackle global warming. To prevent many more species and ecosystems from going extinct, we also need habitat not covered or fragmented by roads, suburbs, and other human artifacts. An ever-increasing fleet of cars—no matter how clean their tailpipes—on ever-spreading grids of pavement is simply not compatible with these goals. But bicycles (and the compact communities that foster bike, bus, and foot travel) can take us where we need to go.

British author H. G. Wells may have summed it up best more than a half century ago: "When I see an adult on a bicycle, I do not despair for the future of the human race."

# The Condom

More than 100 million times today, human beings will have sex. For many millions of couples, this lovemaking will bring great pleasure; yet at least 350,000 people will catch a painful disease from their partners. Today's sex will also make one million women around the world pregnant—about half of them unintentionally.

On this day, one simple object invented centuries ago will spare thousands, if not millions, of people from life-threatening diseases and unwanted pregnancies: the condom. Though not the most widely used method of contraception, the condom is the only one (short of abstinence) that effectively prevents the spread of diseases like chlamydia, gonorrhea, and AIDS. Perhaps one out of six of today's acts of sexual intercourse will involve a condom.

Though it often provokes humor or embarrassment, the lowly condom *is* widely appreciated for all the good it does. Primarily in response to the spread of AIDS, condom sales grew rapidly in the 1980s; Americans, for example, bought 450 million of the prophylactics in 1994. The U.S. Agency for International Development ships an even greater number overseas. Once sold mostly from behind pharmacy counters, condoms are today found in supermarkets, convenience stores, warehouse clubs, catalogs, and even at the drive-through Condom Hut in Cranston, Rhode Island. In much of the world, using condoms has become a norm of responsible sexuality.

The condom is a remarkable little device: weighing in at a fraction of an ounce, it simultaneously fights three of the most serious problems facing humans at the end of the twentieth century: sexually transmitted diseases (STDs), unwanted pregnancies, and population growth. Those are big jobs for a flimsy tube of rubber to accomplish.

AIDS is a global epidemic that now rivals history's worst. Despite the development of new drug treatments, the epidemic is far from over. In 1997, more than 2 million people died of AIDS, nearly 6 million were newly infected with the virus (HIV) that causes the disease, and 31 million people—including 1 out of 100 adults worldwide—lived with HIV or AIDS. In Latin America and the Caribbean, AIDS has overtaken traffic injuries as a cause of death. In a dozen African nations, at least 10 percent of adults are infected with the virus; in Botswana and Zimbabwe, a shocking one out of four adults is HIV-positive.

Even in North America, where health care is better and many AIDS victims can afford expensive antiviral "drug cocktails," the disease remains a major killer. As of 1997, AIDS was still the leading cause of death in Americans 25 to 44 years old. AIDS was at least three times more common (per capita) in the United States than it was in Canada. In both nations, however, minority groups such as blacks, Hispanics, and indigenous people lack access to quality health care and contract the disease at much higher rates.

AIDS is only the tip of the condom, so to speak, of sexually transmitted disease. Unsafe sex is also spreading a range of curable but often deadly ailments (trichomonas, chlamydia, gonorrhea, and syphilis among them) to nearly 400 million victims, including 14 million North Americans each year. There are many ways STDs can kill. Because of the lesions and inflammation they cause, they greatly increase the odds of catching HIV during sex. They also lead to infertility, miscarriages, and stillbirths, as well as pneumonia in newborn infants. Today STDs are the world's leading cause of cervical cancer, and they can lead to fatal hemorrhages during childbirth.

Unwanted pregnancies fuel population growth and all the associated ecological harm, but their toll is heaviest among women themselves. One woman dies each minute because of complications during pregnancy, childbirth, or unsafe abortion. As Mahmoud Fathalla of the World Health Organization observes, "Without fertility regulation, women's rights are mere words. A woman who has no control over her fertility cannot complete her education, cannot maintain gainful employment . . . and has very few real choices open to her."

The United States has a much higher rate of unintended pregnancy than most other developed nations—higher even than dozens of developing nations. More than half of all U.S. pregnancies, and 44 percent of births, are either mistimed (too soon) or unwanted. In Canada, for comparison, 25 percent of births are unintended. Inadequate contraception is not just a Third World issue, as some people think. Especially since a baby born in North America will use roughly 25 times more resources over the course of its life than a baby born in the developing world, population growth is a problem here at home as well as overseas.

While the populations of many European nations are stable or shrinking slightly, the population of the United States has been expanding during the 1990s by 1 percent annually—the equivalent of adding a Kansas every year. Natural increase (births minus deaths)

# No Wonder? Nonoxynol-9

Condoms that include spermicide usually contain nonoxynol-9, a chemical that kills off not only sperm and disease-causing bacteria but the "good" bacteria that keep other bacterial populations in check. As a result, regular use of nonoxynol-9-coated condoms can triple a woman's odds of getting urinary tract infections. Half of all women will have at least one urinary tract infection by the time they turn 30. Each year, there are 7 million cases of urinary tract infection in the United States, with annual health care costs of at least $1 billion.

An unintended pregnancy or a case of gonorrhea has much more serious repercussions than a urinary tract infection, so condom users need to weigh various factors when deciding whether to use spermicide. Those factors include nonoxynol-9's most recently discovered side effects: it can mimic the hormone estrogen in the human body. Research has only begun on hormone-mimicking substances ("endocrine disrupters"), but it is already clear that, even at exceedingly low concentrations, they can cause birth defects, reduced fertility, and other serious disorders.

While researchers learn more about the endocrine-disrupting effects of chemicals like nonoxynol-9, condom users wanting to avoid the health risks associated with spermicide can look for plain lubricated condoms. (Irritation caused by unlubricated condoms can also lead to urinary tract infections.) And to minimize the risk of pregnancy, it is important to follow the instructions on the condom package to prevent spills or tears. The supercautious can also use condoms in combination with another contraceptive for double safety.

is responsible for two thirds of the growth, immigration the rest. Canada is also expanding by 1 percent annually—the equivalent of a Nova Scotia every three years—but with slightly less than half its growth due to natural increase. Immigration has local impacts but, of course, does not add to the total number of people on the Earth, now rising by 83 million people each year.

Contraceptive use has risen in recent years, and population growth has slowed, as women's social and economic status has improved in many nations. Yet contraceptives—especially condoms— need to become much more widely used. By a rough estimate, lovers will employ condoms in only about half of today's 40 million or so acts of sexual intercourse worldwide that risk unwanted pregnancy or disease. A recent survey of Americans with multiple sex partners revealed that those who never use condoms, or use them inconsistently, outnumber those who always use them by 11 to 1. Canadian surveys suggest that as many as half of Canadians with multiple sex partners do not "dress appropriately" every time they have sex.

And contraceptives are far from universally available. Perhaps 500 million couples around the world wish to avoid or delay pregnancy but lack the means to do so. In the United States, federal funding for family-planning services fell by more than 70 percent from 1980 to 1992. The majority of U.S. women of childbearing age have private health insurance, but the only contraceptive covered by many private health plans is surgical sterilization. Similarly, many U.S. insurance companies will pay for Viagra to help a man have sex, but none pay for condoms to enable him to have sex safely.

For family-planning and reproductive health services to be effective, they need to offer women and couples their choice among a variety of contraceptive methods. Condoms lack the side effects of birth-control pills and IUDs and the irreversibility of sterilization, but they have a higher failure rate than these other contraceptives. As many as one out of six women become pregnant during their first year of sex with condoms, but this high rate is due to sporadic—or improper—use. One out of five British men asked to put a condom on a model penis failed to do it right: they tried to unroll the "johnnie" from the inside out. (Great, yet another unsavory slang usage of my first name.) The most important way to improve condoms' effectiveness is to teach people how to use them properly, especially how to avoid spills and tears. With proper and consistent use, condoms' failure rate drops to 2 percent or less of women getting pregnant during their first year of safe sex.

Contraceptive misuse and unintended pregnancies are more frequent in the United States than in other developed nations in part because talk of sex is still taboo in most schools even as it saturates pop culture. Only 10 percent of U.S. students receive comprehensive sex education; one out of four U.S. school districts has an abstinence-only curriculum. In 1997, the U.S. Congress set aside $250 million for local governments to teach that abstinence is the only effective method of birth control and that sex outside of marriage "is likely to have harmful psychological and physical effects."

Abstinence *is* the most effective form of contraception and prevention of sexually transmitted diseases. But try telling that to people having sex 100 million times a day.

The condom is the only sustainable wonder designed to be thrown away after one use. Unlike most disposable goods, condoms *have* to be thrown away, for obvious sanitary reasons. Fortunately, because almost all condoms are made from natural latex (rubber), their ecological impact is much lower than if they were made from synthetic rubber. For example, it takes at least three tons of petroleum to make a ton of synthetic rubber. Synthetic rubber also lacks natural latex's great strength and elasticity, essential qualities for condoms. (And airplane tires, for that matter. All the world's commercial airplanes, and even the space shuttle, roll on tires made of processed tree sap.)

While rubber tapping in the Amazon is environmentally benign, monoculture rubber plantations in Southeast Asia have replaced large areas of tropical forest. And to become a condom, raw latex has to be heated, cured with sulfur (vulcanized), and mixed with other additives before a mandrel (a penis-shaped glass tube) can be dipped into it (twice) to form a condom. Still, whatever impact rubber production has in the world, condoms are responsible for exceedingly little of it. The natural rubber in one car tire is enough to make 1,100 condoms.

Condom packaging does leave much to be desired. A highly (*ahem*) scientific survey conducted in Aisle 8B of the Bartell Drugs downstairs from Northwest Environment Watch's Seattle office revealed that just 1 of 27 types of condoms for sale came in recycled packaging; the rest came in heavily bleached boxes of virgin cardboard. The boxes and the wrappers inside undoubtedly caused more environmental damage than the product they contained. But in the end, condoms' packaging problems are small compared with the good they do by preventing unwanted births and the spread of disease. If all the world's couples used condoms every time they had sex, they'd end up using 100 million condoms a day and 200 tons of rubber, 70 tons of lubricant, and 1,400 tons of packaging.

But that would still pale in comparison with the 5,500 tons of synthetic and natural rubber consumed in one day's worth of tire manufacturing in the United States alone.

Tackling the big-ticket ecological threats to humanity's future—like the climate-altering pollution that rises from all our four-tired vehicles—means stabilizing human numbers at a level the Earth can support. Halting population growth will require, among other things, reducing the poverty and sexual abuse that induce women—in North America and around the world—to bear children. It also requires making condoms and other family-planning and reproductive health services more widely available.

Better funding for government programs that get condoms and other contraceptives into people's hands and educate them on proper use will go a long way toward halting the spread of sexually transmitted diseases and the growth in human numbers. But in the end, the burden falls on individuals and couples to enjoy their sexuality—and plan their families—responsibly. So, to wrap up, use a condom!

# The Ceiling Fan

Here in Seattle, summers are mild, and most houses are cooled by little more than shade trees and cross-breezes. But Seattle is hardly the only place where it's rare for buildings to have air-conditioning. Even in the steamy tropics, air conditioners are the exception, not the norm. For millions of people living near the equator, comfort means simple wooden blades lazily rotating overhead—ceiling fans.

Until fairly recently, fans were the favored cooling device in the United States as well. In 1960, 12 percent of U.S. homes were air-conditioned; as recently as 1973, most American households used only fans and open windows for summertime cooling. Today nearly every new house in the nation comes with forced-air climate control. (Cooling is, not surprisingly, less prevalent in Canada: 29 percent of Canadian households have air-conditioning, up from 12 percent in 1975.) With its low energy prices and three fourths of homes chilling their air, the United States may be the coldest nation in the world each summer—indoors, at least.

Cooling has not come cheap. Air conditioners use up one sixth of electricity in the United States; they tie with refrigerators for demanding the most electricity in U.S. households. On hot summer afternoons, air conditioners consume 43 percent of the nation's peak power load—enough to occupy (and require the construction of) 200 giant power plants, each costing over $1 billion.

Electricity is so familiar that it is easy to forget that the invisible juice flowing out of small sockets in our walls causes acid rain, global warming, salmon extinction, nuclear waste, and various human health problems. Roughly half of North America's electricity comes from burning coal, the dirtiest fossil fuel. Electricity generation emits 35 percent of the United States' climate-changing carbon dioxide and 70 percent of its acid rain–forming sulfur dioxide. Canadian electricity pollutes less—only 15 percent of it comes from coal—but Canada's hydropower and nuclear plants cause plenty of other problems. According to the Rocky Mountain Institute, air-conditioning an average U.S. household sends about three tons of carbon dioxide up power plant smokestacks each year. Cold comfort indeed.

Unfortunately, more and more people are getting chills. American exports of HVAC (heating, ventilating, and air-conditioning) equipment tripled in the past ten years; India's air-conditioning market, among others, has more than doubled since 1988. I can personally report that many movie theaters and taxicabs in Indonesia are so cold they feel like meat lockers. The booming tropical market for air-conditioning is doubly harmful: although production of ozone-depleting chlorofluorocarbons (CFCs) has been banned in industrial nations since 1996, air conditioners and refrigerators sold in developing nations still contain CFCs (and will until 2010). The CFC concentrations—and ozone holes—in the atmosphere are expected to peak by 1999; the ozone layer won't fully repair itself until the twenty-second century.

Everyone deserves to be comfortable. But comfort doesn't have to come at nearly the ecological cost it does today. That's why the ceiling fan is a sustainable wonder: it's an elegant and energy-efficient alternative to air-conditioning and all the problems air-conditioning causes.

Fans cool by creating light breezes that evaporate moisture from the skin. The gentle air circulation from a ceiling fan makes a room as comfortable as one where motionless air is 9°F (5°C) colder. Fans also work their wonders with very little electricity: at highest speed, a ceiling fan uses 50 to 75 watts (as much as one incandescent light-bulb)—less than one tenth the wattage of a medium-sized room air conditioner. At the average U.S. price of electricity, running that fan at its highest speed for 12 hours a day costs about $1.50 a month; running the air conditioner would cost $20 or more.

Much of the time, a ceiling fan will be enough for keeping cool. Even when it's not, using a fan together with an air conditioner can greatly reduce the expense and impact of chilling the air. With a fan going, you can set a thermostat 9°F (5°C) higher and feel just as comfortable—and save about a third off the cooling (and global warming) bill. (Each degree Fahrenheit you turn up the thermostat saves roughly 3 to 5 percent on air-conditioning costs.)

Even before electricity was discovered, people cooled their homes effectively. For thousands of years, people designed their buildings to reject heat with thick, slow-to-heat walls, well-placed windows and vents, and other clever innovations. Temperatures in twelfth-century Anasazi pueblos, for example, varied only one fourth as much as the harsh desert conditions outside their thick adobe walls. Environmentally attuned building design, in tandem with other energy-efficiency measures, can reduce or eliminate the need for air-conditioning, even in extreme climates. An experimental (but normal-looking) tract house commissioned by Pacific Gas and Electric in Davis, California—where summer temperatures reach 110°F (43°C)—achieves standard comfort levels with *no* air conditioner. Because of good design and materials, including well-positioned and superinsulated windows, a light-colored roof, and efficient appliances, the family living there pays 80 percent less in energy bills than their neighbors do. On top of the energy savings, the house itself—if its construction methods were widely practiced—would cost less than a typical tract house today.

Air-conditioning is only one of many areas where we pay far too high a price—in dollars and pollution—because we let energy go to waste. Practically everything that we use energy for—cooling, heating, lighting, transporting, communicating, manufacturing, you name it—can be accomplished as well or better with much less energy. In their book, *Factor Four: Doubling Wealth, Halving Resource Use*, Ernst von Weizsäcker of Germany's Wuppertal Institute and Amory and Hunter Lovins of the Rocky Mountain Institute illustrate 50 examples where energy and material inputs can be profitably cut by at least a factor of four (75 percent) with no sacrifice in what the energy and materials were being used for. It's an exciting book. At last, someone is promoting reforms of a magnitude befitting global ecological problems, as well as proving how eminently feasible, even attractive, such alternatives are.

Multiplying energy efficiency severalfold is key to saving the world's climate; it may also be the only hope for most developing nations to achieve a decent level of prosperity in a world of limited—and increasingly degraded—resources. The whole world can have comfortable, well-lit indoor spaces, hot water, chilled foods, and other conveniences of modern life—but we can't all have leaky buildings, poorly designed appliances, and all the harmful power

# No Wonder: Halogen Floor Lamps

Lighting consumes one fifth of all U.S. electricity—one fourth if you include the air-conditioning energy used to take away the heat generated by the lights. As Amory and Hunter Lovins of the Rocky Mountain Institute write, incandescent lamps "are actually electric heaters that happen to emit 10 percent of their energy as light."

Money- and energy-saving compact fluorescent lights are widely available, yet they are not as widely used as their energy-guzzling competitors. Since the early 1990s, halogen floor lamps—which are basically 700°F (400°C) electric heaters that emit 5 percent of their energy as light—have taken the lighting market by storm. The 40 million halogen floor lamps in the United States use five times more power annually than is generated by wind and solar power combined. The wildly popular lamps now consume 1 percent of the nation's electricity, more than wiping out the energy saved by compact fluorescent bulbs.

Safety concerns may curtail the halogen craze: they've been implicated in nearly 200 fires in the United States and banned from numerous college campuses. Many universities have begun replacing them in dorms with compact fluorescent floor lamps, which provide the same or more light with low-temperature bulbs that use one sixth the electricity and last five times as long as their halogen equivalents.

plants that go with them. With energy used efficiently, there's no need for anyone to go through energy like the average North American, nearly six times faster than the global average.

Buildings are a good place to start improving energy efficiency: they use a third of the energy and two thirds of the electricity in the

United States, the world's biggest energy consumer. Because power plants typically convert 40 percent or less of the energy in the fuel they burn to electricity (the rest is sent up a smokestack or down a drainpipe as waste heat), electricity saved in a home or business can save two to three times as much energy behind the scenes. In addition, making lights and appliances more efficient saves energy doubly: reducing the waste heat they generate reduces room-cooling needs as well.

From skylights and ceiling fans to basement insulation, there are hundreds of ways to conserve energy in any given building. Many local utilities provide free or discounted energy audits to help homeowners determine their energy-saving priorities, but funding for these services is being cut. Electric utilities are gutting their investments in energy efficiency, renewable energy, and low-income assistance as they gear up for deregulated competition over customers. Deregulation might be a boon for energy consumers—many will soon be able to choose their power providers—but it will only benefit the environment if lawmakers ensure that utilities maintain a reasonable level of investment in efficiency and renewables.

Though all kinds of efficiency improvements can be made at a profit, various institutional barriers, habit, and backward economic incentives wed our economy to its wasteful ways. With energy so cheap in North America—highly subsidized and not held accountable for the costly damages it causes—few people bother to conserve it. Green taxes on energy, matched with tax cuts on our paychecks or purchases, would reverse those incentives and give individuals and businesses more reason to improve the energy efficiency of everything from their washing machines to their factories. A tax shift would reward businesses that downsize their unproductive kilowatt-hours instead of their workforces. And individuals would profit by choosing energy misers when buying new light-bulbs, appliances, and homes.

Better energy efficiency doesn't necessarily mean investing in new technologies. It often simply means adopting the ones already at hand: 60 percent of American households have at least one ceiling fan; almost a quarter have three or more fans. Resorting to air-conditioning only when fans can't handle the job alone can yield bigger energy savings than investing in a new cooling system. Other simple measures—such as kicking off your shoes, sipping a cool drink, or growing shade trees around the house—are all energy-efficient ways of cooling down. Because an office worker feels about 5°F (3°C) warmer in a coat and tie than in a short-sleeve shirt, simply allowing employees to dress casually can save an office $150 per employee in cooling and electrical equipment costs and $5 per employee in annual air-conditioning bills.

What's ironic—or perhaps tragic—about the world's environmental undoing is that so little of it does anyone any good. So much of the coal fumes blown out of smokestacks serves only to cool or warm the air *outside* buildings' leaky windows and walls. So many dams power only heat coming out of lightbulbs or heat-generating friction in poorly built appliance motors. So many atomic reactions provide heat that no one ever feels: studies show that in most American households, no one bothers to adjust the thermostat when the home is empty or when everyone is asleep. The flip side of this irony is that doing the right thing—using energy efficiently the way a ceiling fan does—is no sacrifice; on the contrary, it's financially and emotionally rewarding. With a ceiling fan spinning overhead, there's no need to feel uncomfortable about making ourselves comfortable.

# The Clothesline

Susan Warner lives in the middle of a rain forest—in Juneau, Alaska—but she loves hanging clothes up to dry. "I *like* seeing laundry," the working mother of one explains. "Last weekend, our neighbor had pretty colored sheets hanging in the wind, and I really appreciated it. Where my parents live now in California, they're not even *allowed* to use clotheslines." It rains every other day in Juneau, and hypothermia-inducing drizzle seems to threaten year-round, yet Sue and husband Ken have no dryer in the laundry room of their 1913 home in Juneau's downtown historic district. Sue relies mostly on foldable wooden racks in her basement. "Why would I want a dryer?" she asks. "I mean, clothes dry by themselves!"

Clotheslines do require more time and effort than dryers, but I figure if Susan can line-dry her clothes in North America's rainiest city, anyone can. She loves clotheslines and clothes racks because they're simple, silent, and completely nonpolluting. They take few materials to manufacture and require no electricity or fuel to operate. Line-dried clothes smell fresh and have no static, and people who air their drippy laundry outside get to notice the weather, which flowers are in bloom, and who their neighbors are.

Ken Baldwin contributed to this chapter.

By letting the sun and wind do for free what dryers need electricity or gas for, clotheslines also save money. Diehards like Sue avoid the expense of a new dryer, but even dryer owners save money by hanging clothes on the line whenever time and weather permit. In a typical home, the clothes dryer uses much less electricity than central air-conditioning or a refrigerator but more than any other appliance. Feeding the dryer electricity will cost about $85 annually, and $1,100 over its lifetime. Because clothes last longer when they're spared a tumble dryer's heat and wear and tear, clotheslines protect the $1,000 that the average American household invests in new clothing each year. Just look in any dryer's lint trap to see the damage done as clothes shake and bake.

Sadly, clotheslines have fallen out of fashion. The automatic dryer, first manufactured in 1939, started becoming popular in the postwar appliance frenzy of the 1950s. In 1960, less than a fifth of American households, and only an eighth of Canadian households, had automatic dryers. Today three fourths of both nations' households have dryers; only 15 percent of U.S. households even occasionally line-dry their clothing. Many apartment buildings and homeowners' associations have gone so far as to ban clotheslines entirely. They apparently fear that sweet-smelling, freshly washed clothes billowing in the sun will somehow bring down their property values.

Clotheslines—and the energy that makes them work—get no respect. Although solar, wind, geothermal, and biomass power officially contribute less than 2 percent to current global energy supplies, we already use these renewable energy sources—the sun, above all—in unacknowledged ways. Solar designer-philosopher Steve Baer has dubbed this "the clothesline paradox": dry your laundry in an electric dryer, and the electricity you use is counted in conventional energy statistics, but dry your clothes on a clothesline instead, and the solar and wind energy you harness is never measured. The sun, of course, also heats our entire world from about 400°F (240°C) below zero to livable temperatures, but we only count as "energy use" the energy required to heat or cool the insides of our buildings the last few degrees to room temperature.

The decline and fall of the clothesline have come at an environmental price. A typical North American family of four does about six loads of laundry a week and devotes about 5 percent of its annual electricity use to the dryer. With the mix of fuels burned to generate U.S. electricity, the average household dryer puts almost a ton of climate-damaging carbon dioxide into the atmosphere per year. (The same dryer in Canada would send up less than 500 pounds [about 200 kilograms] of carbon dioxide but create more river damage and nuclear waste.) The heating coils in most dryers (20 percent of American dryers heat with gas) require about three kilowatt-hours of electricity per load, enough to read by the light of a 60-watt bulb for two days or work on a laptop computer for a week.

Like many appliances, new dryers are more efficient than old ones. Moisture sensors in today's dryer drums can save about 15 percent of the energy used when relying on a dryer's timer. On the horizon is the microwave clothes dryer, which offers a potential 28 to 40 percent savings. But none of these technologies can match the 100 percent savings of the simple clothesline.

By drawing on the wind and sun, the clothesline avoids all the environmental impacts of electricity and natural gas. The clothesline is one of an array of technologies—from the ancient to the avant-garde—that fight global warming, acid rain, nuclear waste, and a host of other ills. These pervasive energy-related problems have twin solutions: using energy more efficiently (see "The Ceiling Fan," page 27) and shifting as quickly as possible to renewable energy sources.

Fortunately, renewable energy is superabundant, and the cost of tapping into it is falling rapidly. In an hour and 15 minutes, the Earth receives as much energy in the form of sunlight as humans officially use in a year. If American rooftops were covered with solar shingles, they could supply half to three quarters of the country's present energy needs; winds in the United States are capable of supplying roughly one and a half times all the electricity used nationwide. Capturing a tiny fraction of these abundant resources would go a long way toward meeting the world's energy demands.

The clothesline is only the most obvious way to tap into the renewable energy all around us. Considering the energy used to heat water, washing a load of clothes in warm water actually uses about twice as much energy as heating the load in a dryer. (Water heating accounts for nearly 20 percent of home energy use in the United States.) Rooftop solar water heaters use the sun to heat and natural convection to pump water into a home water tank. It can take several years to recoup the initial costs of these simple but pricey systems, depending on energy prices and how much sun smiles on your home. Israel has installed nearly a million solar hot water heaters, which now provide hot water for four out of five Israeli homes.

Homes and businesses can be (and are) heated, cooled, lit, and powered by solar energy in its various forms. "Passive solar" design, such as well-placed windows and overhangs that let in warm light from the low-hanging winter sun but not from the high summer sun, can minimize or eliminate the need for heating and air-conditioning. Even in the cloudy Pacific Northwest, passive solar design can supply 65 percent of a home's space heating. As an ad for Velux windows says of sunlight, "It traveled millions of miles to get here. The least you can do is let it in."

Half a million homes worldwide generate their own solar power with photovoltaic (PV) cells, wafer-thin semiconductors that turn light into electricity. PVs are probably most familiar as the power source for many handheld calculators. Solar cells provide a minuscule share of the world's electricity, but their sales have nearly tripled since 1990. Production costs are dropping rapidly as sales multiply, though PV-generated power still costs too much to compete except in remote locations. Much like related computer chip technology, PV technology is advancing swiftly, and major corporations like British Petroleum and Shell are making multimillion-dollar investments. Still, it's likely that, as clothes dryers and energy-inefficient buildings replace clotheslines and passive solar practices, solar energy's *real* share of world energy use is declining.

The circulation of the atmosphere is driven by differences in the amount of solar energy reaching different parts of the Earth. Humans have harnessed energy in the resulting winds with windmills, sails, and other technologies for millennia. As in passive solar design, buildings can be designed (and operated) to take advantage of the prevailing air movements. Opening the windows on opposite sides of a house harnesses wind energy for good cross-ventilation. A "thermal chimney"—which can be created simply by opening first-floor windows and a window at the top of the stairs to the second floor—draws breezes through the house because warm air rises and is replaced by cooler air below.

A more sophisticated means of capturing wind energy, wind turbines convert wind into electricity. Wind power provides less than 1 percent of world electricity, but capacity is expanding at a rate of 25 percent per year, making wind the world's fastest-growing energy source. The cost of wind-generated electricity in the United States has dropped from 25 cents per kilowatt-hour in 1984 to less than 5 cents per kilowatt-hour today, making it competitive with coal and cheaper than nuclear power. In some regions of Europe, wind power already supplies 5 to 10 percent of electricity.

The United States was the world leader in installed wind power until recently, but pressures to cut costs in the newly deregulated utility industry have led many electric utilities to slash their spending on renewable energy and conservation. Canada, despite having vast prairies, windswept coasts, and a land area second only to Russia's, has only one major wind farm in operation.

Modern wind turbines are much quieter than their predecessors; most people cannot hear them 300 yards away. Some nature lovers fear that wind farms will endanger bird populations, but recent studies in Europe have concluded that well-designed and well-sited wind farms pose little risk to birds. A study for the Danish Ministry of the Environment found that power lines, including those leading to wind farms, endanger birds much more than do wind turbines themselves.

Realizing the promise of renewables will take more than concerned individuals using clotheslines or rooftop solar panels. Building market volumes enough to bring prices down will require large-scale investments. The U.S. Department of Energy recently launched a "million roofs" initiative aimed at installing solar systems on a million U.S. buildings, but the program has stalled for lack of funding. By contrast, the Japanese government recently launched the largest-ever initiative to jump-start markets in solar PV cells, providing $130 million in 1997 to put solar panels on 9,000 homes.

This initiative alone increased the global market for solar cells by roughly a third. In response, companies such as Sharp, Sanyo, and Canon began major scale-ups in their PV production facilities. The government hopes to have installed solar cells on 70,000 Japanese homes by the year 2000.

Shifting to renewable energy sources and reducing the amount of energy we waste are the keys to reducing the bloated impacts of industrial nations on the atmosphere. To stabilize the world's climate, industrial nations will also need to help provide alternatives to fossil fuels in the developing world. Otherwise, the two billion people in the world without electricity, and the many who have a little but want more, will turn to the world's vast supplies of heavily polluting coal to meet their energy needs. And books like *Our Landscapes Are from Mars, Our Climate Is from Venus* will top the best-seller lists of the twenty-first century.

While European nations have begun taxing fossil fuels to discourage their combustion, U.S. and Canadian government policies make these fuels artificially cheap, discouraging investment in renewable alternatives. The United States provides direct subsidies and tax breaks for fossil fuels to the tune of $18 billion per year; Canada provides Can$8 billion (about US$6 billion) worth of tax incentives (a whopping Can$290 per Canadian) to its oil and gas producers.

In short, if investors and energy users had to pay (through taxes or other mechanisms) for all the pollution, health problems, and climate change caused by fossil fuels, renewables would quickly take over the world energy market. Clotheslines would spring up in North American backyards faster than dandelions, and energy-efficient front-loading washing machines—which use less hot water than top-loading machines and make drying easier with their faster spin cycles—would quickly turn today's top-loaders into an icon of wasteful decades past.

Individuals have usually lacked the power to choose renewable energy (except with actions like drying clothes in the sun), but that may soon change. Deregulation of the utility industry, if it doesn't extinguish renewable providers first, may soon allow electricity customers in much of North America to choose "green" power, often for a few dollars more per month. Several companies began offering "coal- and nuke-free" electricity at premium prices to test markets in 1998. Yet not everything is as it seems in the world of green marketing. The Bonneville Power Administration is marketing power from salmon-killing dams in the Columbia River basin to California customers under the name Environmental Resource Trust, even as many environmentalists in the Northwest advocate tearing down four of those dams to save endangered salmon runs. Go figure.

Running through this tangle of policy, economics, and technology, the simple clothesline proves that we can meet our needs without overwhelming the Earth. In 1997, when student activists at Vermont's Middlebury College wanted to protest nuclear energy, they organized students across New England to hang their sheets out on clotheslines as a symbolic protest. Their simple message: sustainability can begin in our own backyards.

# Pad Thai

I am weak. Almost every time I go to a Thai restaurant, I order the same thing. Though I love peanut sauces and hot-and-sour soups and curries over rice, the siren song of *pad thai* inevitably draws me in. For those who don't live near trendy towns like Seattle where Asian restaurants abound, *pad thai* means simply "Thai noodles." This savory, slightly sweet dish, one of the most commonly eaten foods in Thailand, is a mainstay of Thai restaurants everywhere. Flat rice noodles are sautéed with garlic and a complex balance of sweet, sour, salty, and spicy flavorings. Scattered through the tangle of seasoned noodles are a variety of vegetables and usually one's choice of chicken, shrimp, or tofu. The best *pad thai* includes traditional ingredients such as fish sauce, tamarind, and palm sugar, but it can be made (quite palatably, believe it or not) with ketchup as a key ingredient. I've never met a *pad thai* I didn't like.

I'm not alone in my feelings for Thai noodles. Food industry watchers have dubbed Asian cuisine a major trend of the 1990s, as noodle houses and other Asian restaurants crop up in hip downtown neighborhoods and suburban food courts across North America. Sales at Asian restaurants in the United States nearly doubled from 1984 to 1995, while mainstream supermarkets and decidedly nonethnic restaurant chains like TGI Friday's and the Cheesecake Factory increasingly feature foods and dishes from the Pacific Rim.

*Pad thai* is a sustainable wonder because, like most Asian food, it consists mainly of rice and vegetables, is nutritious and low in fat, and has less environmental impact than the typical American meal. Most Asians are meat eaters, but as a whole, they eat far less of it than Americans do. The average person in Thailand eats less than a fifth as much meat as the average American. Thais eat slightly more fish than Americans, but what they really eat more of is rice—more than a pound apiece every day. (The average American consumes just 24 pounds [11 kilograms] of rice in an entire year, about one sixth of it in the form of beer.) With 3 billion Asians relying on rice as their main staple, it is the world's most popular food.

Asians—half the world's people—get about 10 percent of their calorie intake from animal products. Just as meat is, well, the "meat" of the Western diet, Asian diets—and cultures—are built around rice. "Have you eaten your rice today?" is a polite greeting in China, Korea, and Bangladesh. In Japanese and Chinese, the three meals are called morning, afternoon, and evening rice. In the United States, by contrast, a good meal—or an in-depth analysis—is "meaty," and one of the most memorable political sound bites in recent times was Walter Mondale's "Where's the beef?"

The most extensive study of diet and disease ever undertaken has shown that the Asian grain-based diet is much healthier than its meaty North American counterpart. The China-Oxford-Cornell Diet and Health Project tracked the eating habits of 6,500 people throughout rural China and found that the Chinese consume, on average, two thirds less fat, one fifth less protein, and more than three times as much fiber as Americans. As a result, the Chinese have far lower cholesterol levels and much lower incidences of chronic illnesses such as heart disease, stroke, diabetes, and breast and colon cancer. While the excess fat that usually comes with animal protein is the main culprit behind these "diseases of affluence," excess protein itself raises the risk of osteoporosis by causing the kidneys to excrete calcium. Even though dairy products are almost unknown in China, osteoporosis is uncommon there.

Investigators also noted China's rising rates of disease as many upwardly mobile Chinese abandon their traditional low-fat, low-meat diets for meatier fare. Just as Asian foods are spreading across America, American foods are, unfortunately, spreading across Asia. *Hanbao* (hamburgers) and *jishi hanbao* (cheeseburgers) are popular in Beijing, home of the world's largest McDonald's, with 1,000 employees and 29 cash registers. Per capita meat consumption in China has doubled in the 1990s to 105 pounds (48 kilograms) annually. Thais have not moved up the food chain as rapidly (they only eat 46 pounds [21 kilograms] of meat per person), but *farang* (Western) food is making inroads in Thailand as well.

For populations not conditioned to eating large amounts of meat, even small increases in meat consumption can lead to sizable increases in chronic disease. A comprehensive study by the World Cancer Research Fund and the American Institute for Cancer Research recently concluded that diet causes more cancer worldwide than any other factor, including smoking. It speculated that the entire health budgets of many developing countries could soon be consumed by cancer treatment alone because of the expected increase in cancer cases brought by increasing affluence and meat eating. Colin Campbell of Cornell University, one of the directors of the China project, predicts that as many people alive in the world today will die prematurely because of overconsuming animal products as will die from smoking.

Many of those diet-induced deaths will occur in the United States, where people eat more meat (260 pounds [120 kilograms] a year on average) than any other nation on Earth. The typical North American diet is unhealthy both for what's in it and for what's missing. On any given day, nearly half of Americans eat no fruit and nearly a quarter eat no vegetables, depriving their bodies of needed vitamins, fiber, and cancer-fighting antioxidants. In tandem with sedentary lifestyles, fat-laden diets leave the majority of Americans overweight and more than one in five of them clinically obese. (In Canada, where per capita meat consumption runs about 210 pounds [95 kilograms] per year, more than one in eight adults are obese.) Diseases attributable to meat consumption cost the United States at least $29 billion annually in medical costs and billions more in lost productivity.

Even so, the North American diet has improved over the past couple of decades. Americans got 33 percent of their calories from fat in 1994, down from 40 percent in the late 1970s. Red meat consumption in the United States peaked in 1976 and has been falling since then (poultry replaced beef as the most popular meat in 1987). Canadians' average red meat consumption has fallen 25 percent over the past 20 years.

But fat intake remains much higher than the 20 percent of calories advocated by the American Cancer Society and more than twice as high as the 10–15 percent of calories suggested by the China-Oxford-Cornell study as necessary to prevent most cases of diseases of affluence. Substituting white meat for red meat and buying skim milk won't cut our fat intake by half or more. Doing that will require eating lower on the food chain, treating meat as a delicacy rather than a staple. In short, it will mean more meals centered around grains and vegetables, like *pad thai*.

Not that there's anything inherently wrong with eating meat or raising livestock: for most of their history, chickens, cows, and pigs have been raised as an ecologically appropriate sideline to crops, turning plants that humans cannot eat into food that we can. Even today, most sustainably run farms include livestock as an essential part of their operations. The animals recycle nutrients by digesting cover crops, grasses, and crop wastes; their manure, used in moderate amounts, is a valuable natural fertilizer.

But the huge demand for meat in North America—and increasingly around the world—has transformed livestock raising from a sideline niche into the main event. Today, most meat, milk, and eggs in industrial nations are produced by resource-intensive agribusinesses that funnel huge amounts of energy, water, and crops into factory-like facilities that emit both food and waste on an industrial scale.

Agriculture is the leading source of water pollution and the biggest water user in North America, as well as the main force behind soil erosion and the loss of wetlands and grasslands. And livestock are the leading agri-culprit: they eat most of the continent's grain harvest and graze on or eat feed from most of the land area in the United States outside Alaska. Livestock production consumes almost half the energy used in American agriculture; in Canada, farm animals eat over three times more grain than humans do. About seven pounds of grain are needed to produce a pound of boneless, trimmed pork; about three pounds for each pound of chicken; and, depending how much time cattle spend grazing before entering a feedlot, about five pounds for a pound of beef.

It's not surprising that the livestock economy has outgrown its habitat, considering that livestock outnumber humans on this planet more than three to one. (I keep having this Gary Larsonesque image of the world's 13 billion beady-eyed chickens rising up against us to take over the world.) The 7 billion chickens, turkeys, cows, and pigs in the United States alone produce almost 4 million tons of manure per day—about 130 times more than the nation's humans produce. Manure and feed fertilizers together probably contribute a third of the nitrogen and phosphorous released into American waters, nutrients that cause harmful algal blooms and often make well water unsafe to drink. One giant hog farm under construction in Utah will generate more waste than all 2 million people in the state.

Of course, a diet based on grains, fruits, and vegetables is not without environmental impacts. Japan's highly subsidized rice farmers, for example, so saturate their paddies with pesticides that many rural Japanese children have never seen a firefly. Rice farming is also one of the world's largest sources of methane emissions, which are second only to carbon dioxide emissions in their impact on the global climate.

Plants as well as animals need to be raised more sustainably (see "The Ladybug," page 61). Yet in almost every category of environmental concern associated with agriculture—water and energy consumption, erosion, overgrazing, pollution, even methane emissions—grains and vegetables are hands-down winners over livestock. A pound of beef produced in the United States sends about a half pound of methane into the atmosphere—the greenhouse equivalent of burning half a gallon of gasoline. That's six times more than what a pound of U.S. rice generates. Globally, livestock and their manure top rice paddies as sources of methane.

The problems arising from animal agriculture are vexing enough with just one in four people worldwide eating a meat-centered diet. There's no way the world can support 6 billion—much less a future

8 to 12 billion—heavy beef eaters. For everyone in the world today to eat an American-style diet—with 260 pounds of meat annually—farmers would have to grow nearly *three times* as much grain as they do now.

The staggering waste of crops required by the North American diet does not mean that world hunger is caused by people eating Big Macs. Most of the world's 840 million malnourished people simply lack the money and land to buy or grow enough food. Eating lower on the food chain won't do much to solve the problem of global hunger; only a frontal attack on the root causes of poverty can do that. Yet as the number of mouths to feed keeps growing, land now used to grow feed crops could be needed to fight hunger in the future. Asian-style diets make the most of increasingly scarce cropland: it takes about an acre of pasture and cropland to support the average Chinese person's diet, while it takes about four acres to support the average American.

Restoring livestock to their original niche as nutrient recyclers and occasional sources of protein will require a two-pronged effort: dietary changes at home and policy changes in the world's halls of power. Revising the farm programs that subsidize feed crops and penalize sustainable growers would encourage many farmers to change what and how they produce from the land. As mentioned in other chapters, reducing energy subsidies and shifting taxes onto energy use or greenhouse gas emissions would also tilt the playing field toward less energy-intensive foods and agricultural techniques. Reforms such as these can help us move away from our current system of having crops processed (and largely wasted) by the digestive tracts of animals and toward a farm economy where live-

# Do-It-Yourself *Pad Thai*

This recipe is based on *Real Thai: The Best of Thailand's Regional Cooking* by Nancie McDermott (San Francisco: Chronicle Books, 1992); many other *pad thai* recipes are available at *www.cs.unca.edu/~stigle/padthai.html*.

| | |
|---|---|
| 8 oz rice noodles | 1 lime, quartered |
| 4 tbsp vegetable oil | 4 tbsp chopped peanuts |
| 2 tbsp chopped garlic | 2 cups bean sprouts |
| 4 oz broccoli or other chopped vegetables | 8 slender green onions, sliced diagonally |
| 2 tbsp Thai fish sauce (or soy sauce in a pinch) | Chili paste or powder (to taste) |
| 4 tsp palm or brown sugar | 1 lightly beaten egg (optional) |
| 1 tbsp white vinegar | 4 oz tofu, seafood, or meat (optional) |

Soak noodles in warm water for about 30 minutes. Meanwhile, prepare all remaining ingredients and place next to wok. When noodles are limp and white, drain and place by wok. In 1 tablespoon of oil, sauté the garlic until golden. Add the tofu or meat; brown; set aside. Add vegetables and egg to wok and scramble or cut egg into strips as it fries; set aside. Add remaining 2 tablespoons of oil, heat for 30 seconds, and add the semisoft noodles. With a spatula, spread noodles into a thin layer and turn frequently as they cook. Add the fish sauce, sugar, vinegar, chili, and juice of half a lime; turn the noodles a few more times. Add most of the green onions, peanuts, and sprouts (save the rest for garnish) and any precooked ingredients; cook for one minute. Remove from heat and garnish with remaining ingredients. Serves two.

stock eat little except crop scraps from farms and grass from well-managed lands where more valuable crops cannot be grown.

Shifting toward a diet composed of dishes like *pad thai* can cut the environmental impact of our food down to size. If I substitute a serving of grain-fed chicken with a grain product like rice or pasta, I've halved my food's impact. I'll do even better—for the environment and for my health—if I replace a serving of red meat with grains or vegetables. Grains, fruits, vegetables, and beans are almost always lower in fat (especially artery-clogging saturated fat) than meats.

The three most popular "ethnic" foods in North America (Italian, Mexican, and Chinese) are, generally speaking, based on grains (think pasta, tortillas, and rice). In their unadulterated forms, at least, they incorporate less meat than American or Canadian food. For years, health experts have basically been advising North Americans to eat like peasants: *paisanos* of southern Italy or Mexican *campesinas* eat much less meat than restaurant goers in America.

Yet you don't have to have exotic tastes or access to ethnic restaurants to enjoy plant-based foods. Some of the most familiar American foods, like chicken noodle soup, baked potatoes, or peanut butter and jelly, are skimpy on animal products and environmental impact. Even macaroni and cheese (which is practically Canada's national food: Canadians eat more "Kraft Dinner" than people anywhere else) fills the bill (but ignore the box's instructions: to lower the fat content, skip the butter). The key is to restructure your meals, one meal at a time: try putting rice, pasta, bread, or vegetables at the center of the dish and add meat for flavoring, not for substance. Or try going meatless a couple of days a week. Whatever you do, remember that our choices matter: what we pick up with our forks and chopsticks affects our world as surely as it affects our bodies.

# The Public Library

Look out from any window at the Renton Public Library and you'll see at least four lanes of traffic racing through the center of this industrial suburb south of Seattle. But look down and you may see flashes of red and green magic, the muscular dance of sockeye salmon spawning in shallow water. Renton's library straddles the 80-foot-wide Cedar River—home to Washington's largest sockeye run. It's not exactly an idyllic setting, and the building's 1966 architecture is boxy and a bit drab. But, unlike perhaps any other library, it's a terrific place for watching salmon.

Libraries are also great places for saving salmon. Nobody ever built a library to save an endangered species, but that's one of the things libraries do best. By making books, periodicals, and other materials available for an entire community to share, a library makes thousands of personal copies unnecessary. By reducing the demand for paper, a library saves forests from logging and rivers from logging-road erosion; it saves the places where salmon swim and spawn from pulp mill effluent and the electricity demands of paper mills and printers. The average North American library lends out 100,000 books a year but buys fewer than 5,000, saving nearly 50 tons of paper and 250 tons of greenhouse gas emissions in the process—in short, fighting the habitat loss and pollution that endanger so many species.

Books, of course, are wonders in themselves: if more people could and would read, the world would undoubtedly be a better place. But the substance that the printed word arrives on—paper—carries a high ecological price tag. Growth in packaging, advertising, office paper, and various forms of publishing has doubled global paper consumption in the past 20 years, sending more chain saws into the world's forests and a witches' brew of chemical pollutants into its rivers and bays. Despite increased paper recycling, pulp and paper mills digest about 40 percent of the global timber harvest. A relatively small number of consumers in wealthy nations use most of the world's paper: the United States alone, with less than 5 percent of world population, consumes 31 percent of the world's paper production.

Fortunately, books and other paper products can be enjoyed at a fraction of their current ecological impact if they are given second chances at life. I'm *not* talking about recycling. Recycling is great—don't get me wrong—but it doesn't deserve its status as poster child for ecological living. You've probably heard the mantra "reduce, reuse, recycle," but you may not have known that these imperatives are listed in priority order: recycling is only a bronze medalist in environmental protection.

To produce a book of 100 percent recycled paper—like the one in your hands—a paper mill uses about 60 percent of the energy and generates half the solid waste, one third the greenhouse gases, and 95 percent of the effluent of a mill producing the average U.S. book. To produce "100 percent reused" library books, paper mills (and printing presses) use zero energy and generate zero pollution, since reuse bypasses the production stage altogether.

On average, Americans each buy some eight books a year and borrow about six from a library. (Canadians each buy an estimated three books and borrow eight.) Our library readings come at a fraction of the economic and ecological cost of our bookstore purchases. The average U.S. library book is borrowed 2.4 times a year, the average Canadian book 3.4 times. If one of these books lasts even four years, at least ten people will enjoy it during its shelf life, instead of the one or two who might read the same book purchased in a store. In other words, library patrons enjoy reading at one fifth or one tenth the impact of bookstore customers.

To be sure, books are responsible for a small share of paper consumption: packaging, magazines, newspapers, and office paper all use bigger portions of the world's timber supply. But libraries lend out much more than books. The repeated use of any library materials—periodicals, audio and video materials, even computer terminals—makes similar resource savings possible. There's no reason the library concept can't be expanded to include a whole variety of useful items. The liberal outposts of Berkeley, California, and Takoma Park, Maryland, even have tool libraries where local residents can borrow hedge trimmers, ladders, table saws, and more.

Whatever materials they lend, libraries save money by using resources efficiently. Even taking into account the $20 in taxes that the average American pays to support public libraries, he or she saves about $50 a year by borrowing six free books from a library instead of buying them.

All libraries—private, academic, or public—serve as important repositories of knowledge and centers of learning, yet the public library undoubtedly brings the greatest ecological benefits: a book borrowed from a public library is most likely to take the place of a book purchased from a store. Even more, the public li-

brary is the most democratic of institutions: free and open to all
on an equal basis, dedicated to maintaining an informed and liter-
ate citizenry. Libraries also foster a sense of community by bring-
ing together people of all backgrounds and ages into a welcoming
public space, one of North America's most endangered human
habitats.

Despite their profound benefits, many libraries remain under-
funded and unable to maintain the levels and hours of service they
once did. Canadian libraries in particular have struggled with severe
funding cutbacks since the late 1980s. Many U.S. libraries suffered
cutbacks in the antigovernment 1980s, but, on average, their funding since then has slightly outpaced the growth in the populace
they serve. Libraries' respectable track record in the 1990s likely re-
flects popular goodwill toward libraries (as opposed to many other
government programs) and the fact that local voters, rather than
distant elected officials, provide much of their funding. American
voters approved a remarkable 80 percent of library funding refer-
enda in the past ten years.

The United States today has a system of public libraries without
equal in the world primarily because a 1960s spending boom ex-
tended library service into poor and isolated communities. Nonethe-
less, library goers remain disproportionately white and middle- or
upper-class; about two thirds of adults in the United States and in
Canada use libraries each year. Libraries face a wide range of challenges at the close of the twentieth century, many of them revolving
around integrating Internet and other electronic information sources
into their often aged infrastructure. But the central question for public libraries, as historian Michael Harris writes, is whether they "can
survive the serious financial restraints evident today, or whether pub-

lic librarians will retreat to the more efficient and less expensive pattern of serving only the intellectual minority."

At the least, North America's public libraries are better off than many other libraries. Europe's poorly funded public libraries often saddle users with fees, short hours, and closed stacks; as a result, relatively few Europeans are library users. And America's school libraries, much more numerous than public libraries, are often, like public schools themselves, in terrible financial shape. One in four U.S. public schools has no librarian; one in five secondary-school libraries has no world atlas published within the last ten years.

Libraries are only one of many forms of reuse: renting, buying secondhand, and repairing instead of throwing away are all familiar ways people get the most out of scarce goods. The most popular reuse of all may be video renting, with video stores outnumbering public libraries two to one in the United States and consumers renting five times as many videos as they buy.

Checking out a video uses fewer resources than buying one, but it's not necessarily beneficial ecologically: a trip to the video store may only replace a trip to the movie theater or watching a TV rerun while staying home. The average video renter's three-mile drive to reach a favorite store (scary how much industry marketers know about their customers, isn't it?) just about cancels out the petroleum saved in not manufacturing a videocassette. But the popularity of video rentals shows that, if the price and infrastructure are right, North Americans have no problems with reusing stuff.

Business at thrift stores and other sellers of used goods is grow-

# Small Wonder:
# The Interdepartmental Envelope

Those old-fashioned manila envelopes that close with a string are the cutting edge of Earth-friendly packaging. Covered with spaces for writing and crossing out addresses, they are designed to be reused 30 times or more (before being recycled). They put modern recycling—and the shipping industry—to shame.

Overnight shippers in the United States deliver one billion envelopes and boxes annually—one per U.S. citizen per day—practically all of them trashed after one use. Try to reuse one of FedEx's signature "Overnight Letter" envelopes—made of sturdy bleached, unrecycled cardboard with a plastic sleeve glued on—and you'll be told that company policy forbids reuse. Don't even try to recycle it, unless you feel like spending five minutes tearing off all the plastic first. Though most overnight shipping companies have some recycled cardboard in their envelopes and boxes, the only reusable packaging is UPS's new "Next Day Air Letter," which can be used just twice.

In the United States, 90 percent of shipped goods arrive in disposable cardboard boxes. Americans open so many boxes that containerboard, despite its 64 percent recycling rate, is the single largest component of the nation's waste stream. What would the world look like if documents and bulk goods traveled instead in "interdestinational" packaging with crossed-out names tracing each package's dozens of lives?

ing by 15 to 20 percent a year in the United States, much faster than other retail sectors. Once limited mostly to unsavory pawnshops and charity stores full of barely salable merchandise, secondhand stores (like the Yuppie Pawn Shop in Kirkland, Washington) have become popular among middle-class shoppers who love bargains, even if they don't realize that used goods cost the Earth next to nothing. National chains have moved in to capitalize on the popularity of used clothing; for-profit and nonprofit secondhand stores now sell everything from antique furniture to used sporting goods, CDs, and computer software.

Unfortunately, many forms of reuse have fallen out of favor as acquisition has replaced neighborly borrowing and other forms of sharing, and as cheap appliances and semidisposable Scandinavian furniture have replaced durability and repair. I remember the bottles of milk that came with my elementary-school lunches in the 1970s (the foil caps made great tabletop footballs) and the cases of refillable soda bottles that were a constant feature in our kitchen (and cavities that were a constant feature in my teeth). Refillable bottles may seem a nostalgic relic to Americans, but they are alive and well in most other nations. In Canada, over 97 percent of beer bottles are returned for refilling; in Denmark, 99 percent of all soda and beer bottles are refilled. Even including washing, the use of refillables saves 90 percent or more of the materials and energy required to manufacture new bottles.

Reuse gets little attention as an environmental strategy, but it is one of the overlooked shortcuts that can help us quickly move toward an environmentally sound way of life. While industry and government spend millions on recycling campaigns, refillable bottles fight pollution and waste without fanfare and more effectively.

Even as cutting-edge clothing manufacturers advertise their organic cotton and recycled fleece, unassuming thrift stores keep on selling the most ecologically friendly clothing of all. And while others fight noisily over who needs to do what to keep endangered species from disappearing, libraries go quietly about their business of saving rivers and forests—one book, magazine, compact disc, and hedge trimmer at a time.

# The Ladybug

Les bêtes à bon Dieu, the French called them, or les vaches de la Vierge. Creatures of the good God, cows of the Virgin. To the Germans, they were Marienkäfer, Mary's beetles. Legend has it that grape farmers in medieval Europe were besieged by a plague of aphids and prayed for divine intervention. When brightly colored beetles arrived en masse and devoured the aphids, the grateful farmers named them after "Our Lady," the Virgin Mary.

Few farmers rely anymore on the Virgin Mary to save their crops. But the polka-dotted predators known to English speakers as ladybird beetles, or just ladybugs, still protect farms and gardens. Ladybugs are members of a beetle family with an estimated 4,000 species found all around the world. All but 2 of the 450 or so species in North America are considered beneficial because they feed on aphids and other destructive soft-bodied crop eaters. And they feed voraciously. In three to four weeks of life as a larva (resembling a tiny, six-legged black alligator with orange spots), a ladybug will eat 350 or more aphids. A typical adult ladybug will consume 40 to 75 aphids a day, or about 5,000 in its lifetime.

Multiply such an appetite by the huge number of adults in ladybug colonies—a single colony in the California mountains favored by commercial ladybug dealers may contain as many as 40 million adults—and the benefits start adding up. (Always remember your handy conversion factor: 75,000 adult beetles equal one gallon.) Multiply these benefits by the thousands of species that prey on or parasitize crop pests, and it becomes apparent that agriculture—and the human race—is far more dependent on the work of creepy-crawlies than it is threatened by them. While worldwide sales of pesticides total about $30 billion annually, the pest control services provided by the pests' natural enemies are worth an estimated four times that amount.

Yet most farmers have lost their faith in omnipresent, benevolent beings like predatory insects and turn instead to heavy doses of pesticides for their crops' salvation. Unfortunately, pesticides usually work either too well—indiscriminately killing beneficial and harmful organisms alike—or not well enough, since short-lived species like insects often develop resistance to a given chemical in only a few generations. Farmers' victories against targeted pests are frequently overshadowed by the secondary pests they create: formerly innocuous species whose populations explode in the absence of their usual predators. The farmers then end up on a pesticide treadmill, chasing one newly created "pest" after another.

Predators are not the only life-forms harmed by pesticides. By killing the organisms that disperse pollen, decompose wastes, and build soil, pesticides can even harm the plants they are supposed to protect. Soil isn't "dirt" (that's what you get under your fingernails); it's a complex ecosystem whose organisms help produce about a ton of new soil annually per hectare (2.5 acres) of cropland. The fertility of the soil, as well as most plants' ability to draw nutrients from it, depends on the survival of the fungi, bacteria, and animals in it. Many soil organisms are highly sensitive to agricultural chemicals. In the U.S. Midwest, it takes about five years for healthy populations of earthworms to return to crop fields tilled and heavily sprayed with pesticides.

Animals (mostly insects but also birds, bats, and even a gecko) pollinate 90 percent of the world's flowering plant species; wild and semiwild pollinators (as opposed to domesticated honeybees) pollinate 80 percent of the world's major crop species. Some crops depend entirely on specific pollinators. Blueberry farmers in the southeastern United States view native blueberry bees, each of which pollinates about 30 pints (17 liters) of blueberries in its short life, as "flying $50 bills."

But as biologists Stephen Buchmann and Gary Paul Nabhan, authors of *The Forgotten Pollinators*, explain, "nature's most productive workers [are] slowly being put out of business" by pesticides, diseases, exotic species, and loss or fragmentation of their on-farm and off-farm habitats. Heavy spraying aimed at eradicating pesticide-resistant insects from U.S. cotton fields kills so many pollinators that it reduces the United States' annual cotton production by 10 to 20 percent. Aerial pesticide spraying for forest pests in Canada in the mid-1970s killed off so many wild bees that blueberry yields were down for four years afterward.

Despite enormous increases in global pesticide use, the share of crops lost to insects, fungi, and other pests is apparently as high as it was in the Middle Ages. In the United States, more than 500 insects, 270 weeds, and 150 plant diseases are now resistant to one or more pesticides, and farmers have to apply pesticides two to five times to achieve what one application accomplished in the early 1970s. What Rachel Carson wrote in *Silent Spring* in 1962 still holds true: "The chemical war is never won, and all life is caught in the crossfire."

. . .

An ever-growing body of knowledge since Carson's time about the hazards of pesticides has led to bans on some of the worst chemicals. But the average killing power per pound of pesticides applied today is at least as high as it was in the early 1970s, and the total volumes applied are dramatically higher. Farmers in the United States apply more than twice the amount of pesticides in use when *Silent Spring* first awoke the public to the dangers of DDT and other chemicals. Worldwide, five out of six nations continue to allow DDT despite its well-known and persistent toxicity to creatures ranging from ladybugs to suckling infants and their parents.

Concern over the health and ecological effects of conventional agriculture has led a minority of farmers and consumers in Europe and North America to seek a better way. The United States' million-odd acres of certified organic farmland produced $3.5 billion in food sales in 1996—less than 2 percent of the national total. Organic foods account for 1 percent of all food sales in Canada, with much organic produce imported from the United States. Curiously, much of Canada's homegrown organic food (primarily grains and canola oil) is exported to the United States and Europe.

But these figures capture only a fraction of all sustainable farming. Because of the cost and time involved in certification, half or more of organic farmers do not seek to have their farms certified as chemical free. Though it remains small, organic agriculture is one of the fastest-growing sectors of the North American economy. Sales of organic products in the United States have increased 20 percent or more annually throughout the 1990s; the number of acres certified as organic more than doubled from 1991 to 1994. Canada's organic industry is growing by an estimated 24 percent per year.

Organic farming is not the only environmentally benign form of agriculture. Many farmers use integrated pest management (IPM), a preventive approach that includes diligent, hands-on scouting of the abundance of pests and their enemies before resorting to not-so-toxic pesticides or biological controls tailored to a particular field's needs. Consumers Union (publisher of *Consumer Reports*) estimates that roughly one third of U.S. farmers rely primarily on preventive methods of pest control rather than on pesticides, including 4 to 8 percent who rarely or never use the chemicals.

Pesticides get a great deal of public attention because they can pose potent human health risks, but they are not the only or, many would argue, the most important environmental problem of modern agriculture. Agriculture's growing demands for water, fossil fuels, and land take a heavy toll. The loss of fertile soil may be the most serious long-term threat to food security: raising food for the average U.S. citizen erodes away about 15 tons of soil annually. And the most common contaminant in U.S. groundwater is not a pesticide but nitrates—by-products of manure, fertilizers, and food-processing plants.

Farmers apply enormous quantities of nitrogen fertilizer, so much that half of all commercial fertilizer ever made has been applied since 1984. Fertilizers stimulate plant growth, of course, and they have helped world food production keep pace with an expanding population. Yet on many farms, half the fertilizer applied to fields never reaches crops: instead it evaporates, leaches important nutrients out of the soil, or washes into local waterways, where it can feed toxic or oxygen-depleting algal blooms and contaminate drinking water supplies. Farming and other human activities have already more than doubled the amount of nitrogen cycling through the world's ecosystems.

World fertilizer use actually dropped slightly in the 1990s as farmers in many countries discovered that they were applying more fertilizer than was even possible for their crops to absorb. If consumer demand and public policy rewarded growers for skimping on energy-intensive inputs, many more of them would make the effort to precisely calculate, target, and time their spraying of fertilizers, pesticides, and irrigation water.

When farmers *do* use environmentally costly inputs more efficiently, they often reap unanticipated benefits. Lessened pesticide use allows all sorts of beneficial organisms to get back to work; water-conserving techniques save much more than water. Underground drip irrigation systems, for example, can cut in half the water needs of farms using surface irrigation. Because water no longer flows in muddy rows across the field, it also no longer carries soil, nutrients, or pesticides with it into nearby streams. On one well-documented commercial farm in Arizona, drip irrigation enabled plowing and herbicide spraying to be cut in half and nitrogen fertilizer application by 25 to 50 percent. In addition, crop yields increased 15 to 50 percent because water and chemicals were precisely applied at the roots in just the right amounts. Similarly, a study in North Dakota found that the state's sustainable farms end up using one third the energy of its conventional farms.

Growers wanting to rely less on chemicals and more on beneficial insects can leave parts of their properties (like fencerows and highly erodible hillsides) uncultivated to provide habitat for the creatures that pollinate and protect their crops. But farmers trying to shift away from conventional chemical-heavy agriculture are often penalized for doing so. While some government programs encourage sustainable agriculture, many others, including crop insurance and cosmetic and grading standards, reward farmers for continuing to rely heavily on pesticides.

Making North American agriculture more sustainable and allowing ladybugs and other beneficial organisms to work their wonders will require changes in both consumer habits and public policy. In addition to reforming or axing the programs and subsidies that actively encourage unsustainable practices, governments need to support research and education on alternative farming techniques (which, unlike most pesticides and fertilizers, are usually crop and place specific).

Individually, people can shop for organic, IPM, and locally grown produce and avoid using pesticides, chemical fertilizers, or excessive amounts of water in their own lawns, gardens, and homes. But it's worth noting that even an "organic" label does not guarantee ecological purity. At my local grocery store, hothouse tomatoes and bell peppers from nearby British Columbia often appear in the "organic" section. Yet they're not environmentally friendly: heating and fertilizing vegetable crops in hydroponic Canadian greenhouses requires at least ten times the energy of conventional farming in Canada.

It's also worth noting that even ladybugs can have an ecological downside. Two Eurasian species (the seven-spotted and the many-spotted lady beetle) introduced to selected farming regions in the 1970s by the U.S. Department of Agriculture have since spread far and wide, displacing native ladybugs in several states. Even in wilderness areas high in the Washington Cascades, invaders now outnumber native ladybugs. Because store-bought ladybugs often fly away from backyard gardens rather than settle in for a life of heavy aphid consumption, attracting local beneficial insects is often more effective—and less risky ecologically—than buying predators of unknown origin from a catalog.

No species is a pest until someone deems it one, and every species—even those that become pests—is a sustainable wonder, the successful result of millions of years of trial and error (or what biologists call natural selection). The ecosystems of the world are built upon their backs (or exoskeletons, actually, since more than half of all known species are insects; one out of four is a beetle. When the eminent British geneticist J. B. S. Haldane was asked what characteristics of the Creator could be divined from the wonders of evolution, he is said to have replied, "An inordinate fondness for beetles"). It's no overstatement to say that other species—the vast majority of them little appreciated or even unnamed—make our lives possible. In his essay "The Little Things That Run the World," biologist E. O. Wilson points out that ours is a planet where beetle species alone outnumber vertebrates at least seven to one. He posits that if invertebrates were to disappear tomorrow, the human race would probably not last more than a few months.

So it's not just pretty and familiar ladybird beetles that deserve praise and support for helping put food on our tables. Soils exist and plants grow because of the work of whole communities of grotesque or fearsome creatures like earwigs, spiders, and mites as well as millions of other above- and underground organisms that most of us have never heard of, even though we walk through and over their lilliputian habitats every day. If biologists are ever able to discover and name all the species crawling, flying, squirming, and generally consuming one another on this planet, they may find that the world has not seven, but seven million, sustainable wonders.

# Appendix:
## James Bond
### vs. Superheroes

A couple of years ago, Alan Durning and I wrote a book called *Stuff: The Secret Lives of Everyday Things,* which focused on a dozen familiar objects to show why tackling consumption is North America's central environmental challenge. Everyday things pique people's curiosity, and after the book was published, I got to do lots of interviews about consumption and its hidden impacts. When I did a talk show on a top-rated radio station in Vancouver, British Columbia, the host introduced me not as a mild-mannered, mostly desk-bound researcher, but as an "environmental James Bond." She went on to explain how I delved behind the scenes to uncover dark secrets behind ordinary consumer goods. It was funny but absurd: I imagined thousands of Canadians by their radios, picturing me sipping martinis and blowing up oil refineries.

The very idea of an eco-adventure hero seems ridiculous, but perhaps it's not so crazy after all.

Tremendous obstacles must be overcome if humanity and the rest of life on Earth are to thrive in the twenty-first century. It's easy to become intimidated by massive problems like global warming or the wholesale extinction of species. It's also easy to be cynical about politicians' ability to care about anything more than the next election. Yet it's important to remember how powerful each of us can be in effecting change. Because so few people bother to get involved in government beyond voting once every few years, individual voices have much more clout than we might think.

What we forget is how much our voices—and our choices—matter. Each of us, in fact, has power beyond our wildest dreams. I've come to think of our powers, only half facetiously, as superpowers. With the flick of a wrist—reaching for organic produce instead of the conventional stuff next to it at the grocery store—you can stop pesticides from being sprayed hundreds of miles away. That's a reach any superhero would envy. By putting one foot in front of the other—walking or biking to a neighborhood shop instead of driving to the megastore on the outskirts of town—you can stop oil from being drilled in some place like Nigeria or the arctic slope of Alaska. You'll also stop heat-trapping pollution from damaging an entire planet's climate. *An entire planet's climate.*

Although the sustainable wonders themselves deserve praise, it's the steps *we* take—simplifying our lives and advocating for change—that make all the difference. Egypt's pyramids may be great even if no one gazes upon them, but a clothesline or ceiling fan only saves energy if somebody uses it. A ladybug only works its wonders if pesticides don't kill it; pesticides stop getting sprayed when individuals shop and speak out for sustainably produced foods.

In many cases, the biggest obstacle to a more sustainable way of life is simply habit. Yet once people start doing things differently, new practices quickly become second nature—something you do without thinking about it—and the old ways, whether bottle-toting milkmen or lead-tainted gasoline, soon fade into memory. Recycling, for instance, has become routine for many North Americans over the past 20 years. But what would the world be like if bicycle lanes were as common and well used as recycle bins are today? What would the world be like if everyone supported reuse, energy efficiency, renewable energy, contraception, and sustainable foods? We would quickly outflank the eco-villains of overconsumption and overpopulation menacing the world today.

So who needs a James Bond when we can have a world full of superheroes instead?

Reading (or writing) books doesn't make one a superhero. But information is a crucial first step toward action. Take the next step and see what you can do in your own life. The following sources can help you learn about, use, and advocate your favorite sustainable wonders:

### THE BICYCLE

Try bicycling instead of driving somewhere just once a week and see if it doesn't grow on you. Contact the organizations below or visit their web sites, which list hundreds of local groups working to promote bicycling and to make our streets safer for everyone.

Surface Transportation Policy
   Project
1100 17th St. NW, 10th floor
Washington, DC 20036
(202) 466-2636
*www.transact.org*

Better Environmentally Sound
   Transportation
822-510 W Hastings St.
Vancouver, BC V6B 1L8
(604) 669-2860
*www.sustainability.com/best*

*Tip: If you bike regularly, invest in fenders for a rainy day: they're worth it. And always wear a helmet.*


THE CONDOM

Never have unsafe sex. And support organizations working to ensure that no one else has to, either.


Planned Parenthood Federation
  of America
810 Seventh Ave.
New York, NY 10019
(800) 829-PPFA
*www.plannedparenthood.org*

Planned Parenthood Federation
  of Canada
1 Nicholas St., Suite 430
Ottawa, ON K1N 7B7
(613) 241-4474
*www.ppfc.ca*


Zero Population Growth
1400 16th St. NW, Suite 320
Washington, DC 20036
(800) 767-1956
*www.zpg.org*

Childbirth by Choice Trust
344 Bloor St. W, Suite 502
Toronto, ON M5S 3A7
(416) 961-7812
*www2.cbctrust.com/cbctrust/*


THE CEILING FAN AND THE CLOTHESLINE

For understandable, state-of-the-art information on fitting energy-efficient and renewable-energy technologies into your life, contact the Rocky Mountain Institute (RMI). Their many publications include Richard Heede et al., *Homemade Money: How to Save Energy and Dollars in Your Home* (Snowmass, Colo.: RMI, 1995), and the *Home Energy Briefs* series, including "Home Cooling" and "Washers, Dryers, & Miscellaneous Appliances," $2 each or free on line.

Rocky Mountain Institute
1739 Snowmass Creek Road
Snowmass, CO 81654
(970) 927-3851
*www.rmi.org*

*Tip: Cooling and heating are much bigger energy users than lighting—focus on reducing the energy consumed by your furnace, water heater, and cooling appliances before worrying about changing lightbulbs. Insulating your windows, roof, doors, and pipes and reducing the amount of hot water used in showers and washing machines are first-priority items for saving energy in the home.*

To advocate for energy efficiency and renewable energy, join the fight against climate change:

U.S. Climate Action Network
1200 New York Ave. NW,
  Suite 400
Washington, DC 20005
(202) 289-2401
*www.climatenetwork.org/*
  *USCAN/index.html*

David Suzuki Foundation
2211 W 4th Ave., Suite 219
Vancouver, BC V6K 4S2
(604) 732-4228
*www.davidsuzuki.org*

PAD THAI
Families Against Rural Messes' web site is packed with information and links to other groups fighting pollution from confined livestock operations. EarthSave International promotes eating lower on the food chain in the United States and Canada. Or for real hands-on activism, try cooking the *pad thai* recipe on page 50.

Families Against Rural Messes
P.O. Box 615
Elmwood, IL 61529
(309) 742-8895
*www.netins.net/showcase/*
  *megahoglaws/*

EarthSave International
600 Distillery Commons,
  Suite 200
Louisville, KY 40206
(502) 589-7676
*www.earthsave.org*
*www.earthsave.bc.ca*

THE PUBLIC LIBRARY
Join or form a local "Friends of the Library" group. Or contact national library advocacy groups:

Libraries for the Future
121 W 27th St., Suite 1102
New York, NY 10001
(800) 542-1918
*www.LFF.org*

Canadian Library Association
200 Elgin Street, Suite 602
Ottawa, ONT K2P 1L5
(613) 232-9625
*www.cla.amlibs.ca*

THE LADYBUG
Support organic farmers and others who are breaking away from excessive use of chemicals and energy: buy their produce. And support the political fight for better ways to grow our food:

Pesticide Action Network
North America
49 Powell St., Suite 500
San Francisco, CA 94102
(415) 981-1771
*www.panna.org*

Sierra Club of Canada
Pesticides Campaign
412-1 Nicholas St.
Ottawa, ONT K1N 7B7
(613) 241-4611
*www.sierraclub.ca/national/pest/
index.html*

*Tip: Are organics too expensive where you shop? Grow your own, or help advocate policies that will lower the economic and policy barriers to sustainable agriculture.*

# Sources

PROLOGUE: THE DALAI LAMA VS. *BAYWATCH*

Dalai Lama quoted in John Kenneth Galbraith, "Foreword," in Neva R. Goodwin et al., *The Consumer Society* (Washington, D.C.: Island Press, 1997). Motor vehicles per adult based on "Regions at a Glance," in *World Resources 1998–99* (New York: Oxford University Press, 1998), and *Motor Vehicle Facts & Figures 95* (Detroit: American Automobile Manufacturers Association, 1995). Colin J. Campbell and Jean H. Laherrère, "The End of Cheap Oil," *Scientific American*, March 1998, predict that global oil production will begin declining by 2010; for other predictions, see "Petroleum Resources: When Will Production Peak?" in *World Resources 1996–97* (New York: Oxford University Press, 1996).

Consequences of North American–style driving derived from data on energy consumption, carbon dioxide emissions, and population for Canada, the United States, and the world in *World Resources 1998–99*. A 60 percent reduction in carbon dioxide emissions will stabilize atmospheric carbon dioxide concentrations at their current levels, according to J. T. Houghton et al., eds., *Climate Change: The IPCC Scientific Assessment* (Cambridge, U.K.: Cambridge University Press, 1990).

*Baywatch* viewers from *www.baywatch.com*. Most popular series of all time from Bruce Fretts, "Do You Like to Watch?" *Entertainment Weekly*, 8 October 1993. Calories consumed and quotation from Bill McKibben, "A Special Moment in History," *The Atlantic Monthly*, May 1998.

Human influence on global climate from Intergovernmental Panel on Climate Change (IPCC), *Climate Change 1995: The Science of Climate Change* (Cambridge, U.K.: Cambridge University Press, 1996). Forests from Sandra Postel and John C. Ryan, "Reforming Forestry," in Lester R. Brown et al., *State of the World 1991* (New York: Norton, 1991). Mass extinction from Marjorie L. Reaka-Kudla et al., eds., *Biodiversity II: Understanding and Protecting Our Biological Resources* (Washington, D.C.: Joseph Henry, 1997). Water from Sandra L. Postel et al., "Human Appropriation of Renewable Fresh Water," *Science*, 9 February 1996. Vegetation from Peter Vitousek et al., "Human Appropriation of the Products of Photosynthesis," *Bioscience*, June 1986. Grasslands from Till Darnhofer, Desertification Control Program Activity Center, United Nations Environment Programme, Nairobi, Kenya, private communication, 23 May 1991. Chemicals in body fat from Theo Colborn et al., *Our Stolen Future: Are We Threatening Our Fertility, Intelligence, and Survival?—A Scientific Detective Story* (New York: Dutton, 1996).

On the scale of global ecological reform required, see Ernst von Weizsäcker, Amory Lovins, and Hunter Lovins, *Factor Four: Doubling Wealth, Halving Resource Use* (London: Earthscan, 1997); Mathis Wackernagel and William Rees, *Our Ecological Footprint: Reducing Human Impact on the Earth* (Gabriola Island, B.C.: New Society, 1996); and Wolfgang Sachs et al., *Greening the North: A Post-Industrial Blueprint for Ecology and Equity* (New York: Zed, 1998), among others.

## THE BICYCLE

Bicycle-to-car ratio from Lester R. Brown et al., *Vital Signs 1992: The Trends That Are Shaping Our Future* (New York: Norton, 1992). World vehicle production, European cycling rates, and greater cost to support auto traffic from Lester R. Brown et al., *Vital Signs 1998: The Environmental Trends That Are Shaping Our Future* (New York: Norton, 1998). Cyclists in the United States, benefits of bike lanes, short-trip pollution, and senior citizen cyclists from *The Environmental Benefits of Bicycling and Walking*, National Bicycling and Walking Study, Case Study No. 15 (Washington, D.C.: U.S. Dept. of Transportation, Federal Highway Administration [FHWA], 1993).

Canadian bicyclists from "Mode of Transport to Work," *The Daily*, Statistics Canada, Ottawa, 17 March 1998, available at *www.statcan.ca/Daily/*. Canadian fatalities and registered drivers from *Transportation in Canada 1997*, Annual Report (Ottawa: Transport Canada, 1998), available at *www.tc.gc.ca/tfacts/anre1997/*.

Most energy-efficient form of travel from John C. Ryan and Alan Thein Durning, *Stuff: The Secret Lives of Everyday Things* (Seattle: Northwest Environment Watch, 1997). For a thorough comparison of the environmental costs of cars and bicycling, see Ryan and Durning, *Stuff*.

Leading cause of death from *Accident Facts, 1995* (Itasca, Ill.: National Safety Council, 1995); J. M. McGinnis and W. H. Foege, "Actual Causes of Death in the United States," *Journal of the American Medical Association*, 10 November 1993; John Barber, "Mom's Taxi Could Be a Deathtrap," Toronto *Globe and Mail*, 8 March 1995; and *The Global Burden of Disease and Injury Series* (Cambridge, Mass.: Harvard School of Public Health, Center for Population and Development Studies, 1996), executive summary at *www.hsph.harvard.edu/organizations/bdu/*.

Share of trips from *Our Nation's Travel: 1995 NPTS Early Results Report* (Washington, D.C.: FHWA, 1997), available at *www-cta.ornl.gov/npts/*. Three-car households from *Statistical Abstract of the United States 1998* (Washington, D.C.: U.S. Bureau of the Census, 1998). Who can afford vehicles from Ed Ayres, "Breaking Away," *World Watch*, February 1993. China cropland based on Marcia Lowe, *The Bicycle: Vehicle for a Small Planet* (Washington, D.C.: Worldwatch, 1989).

Trip lengths from *Nationwide Personal Transportation Survey: NPTS Databook 1990* (Washington, D.C.: FHWA, 1994), available at *www-cta.ornl.gov/npts/1990/*. "Errandsville" and Dutch children from Barbara Flanagan, "Cyclist's Fix for Cities: Shift Gears," *New York Times*, 22 May 1997.

Tunnels of pollution from *Road User Exposure to Air Pollution: Literature Review* (London: Environmental Transport Association and Institute for European Environmental Policy, 1997).

Bicyclists' death rates in the United States from Susan P. Baker et al., *Injuries to Bicyclists: A National Perspective* (Baltimore: Johns Hopkins University, Injury Prevention Center, 1993), and from T. Ayres et al., "Risk Analysis and Bicycling Injuries," Exponent Failure Analysis Associates, Menlo Park, Cal., November 1998.

Helmets, fatalities, and motorcycle risks from Bicycle Helmet Safety Institute, Arlington, Va., "A Compendium of Statistics from Various Sources," *www.bhsi.org/webdocs/stats.htm*, viewed July 16, 1998.

Safer form of exercise from Ayres et al., "Risk Analysis and Bicycling Injuries." Toll of sedentary lifestyle, "nearly half of recreational riders," Japanese commuters, ISTEA, Dutch roads budget, and H. G. Wells quote from *The National Bicycling and Walking Study: Transportation Choices for a Changing America*, Final Report (Washington, D.C.: FHWA, 1994).

Davis from *Improving Conditions for Bicycling and Walking: A Best Practices Report* (Washington, D.C.: FHWA, 1998). Traffic calming discussed in Andy Clarke and Michael Dornfeld, *Traffic Calming, Auto Restricted Zones, and Other Traffic Management Techniques: Their Effect on Bicyclists and Pedestrians*, National Bicycling and Walking Study, Case Study No. 19 (Washington, D.C.: FHWA, 1993). Speed-fatality link from *Mean Streets: Pedestrian Safety and Reform of the Nation's Transportation Law* (Washington, D.C.: Environmental Working Group and Surface Transportation Policy Project, 1997), available at *www.ewg.org*.

Numbers of registered drivers from American Automobile Manufacturers Association, *Motor Vehicle Facts and Figures 1997*, and from *Transportation in Canada 1996*, Annual Report (Ottawa: Transport Canada, 1996). Livable cities and suburban vs. city driving from Alan Thein Durning, *The Car and the City* (Seattle: Northwest Environment Watch, 1996).

Bike racks from Dave Olsen, "On the Road to Auto-Free Living, Part III: Multimodal Cycling!" *Spoke'n'Word*, newsletter of Better Environmentally Sound Transportation, Vancouver, B.C., spring/summer 1998.

Other sources: International Police Mountain Bike Association, Washington, D.C., "Police on Bikes Fact Sheet," *www.bikeleague.org/ipmba2/factsht.htm*, viewed August 27, 1998; Natural Resources Defense Council, "ISTEA II Passes At Last," *www.nrdc.org/nrdcpro/analys/tristea.html*, viewed July 22, 1998.

THE CONDOM

Daily sexual acts and their implications based on Pramilla Senanayake and Malcolm Potts, *An Atlas of Contraception* (New York: Parthenon, 1995), and on Bill Bremner, University of Washington, Seattle, private communication, 6 March 1998. Daily condom use based on average of figures in Senanayake and Potts, *An Atlas of Contraception*, and in London International Group, London, "Condoms in the Age of AIDS," *www.durex.com/scientific/faqs/material.html*, viewed March 25, 1998.

Condom sales and condom use of Americans with multiple sex partners from "How Reliable Are Condoms?" *Consumer Reports,* May 1995. USAID from Paula L. Green, "Condom Companies in U.S. Eye Sales Growth Abroad," *Journal of Commerce,* 28 March 1995. Widespread availability from Marcia Mogelonsky, "Bye-Bye Birth Control," *American Demographics,* January 1996.

AIDS among Canadian minorities and condom use of Canadians with multiple sex partners from Eleanor Maticka-Tyndale, "Reducing the Incidence of Sexually Transmitted Disease through Behavioural and Social Change," *Canadian Journal of Human Sexuality,* June 1997, available at *www.hc-sc.gc.ca/main/lcdc/web/publicat/cjhs/cjhs2.html*.

Global toll of HIV and AIDS from *The World Health Report 1998* (Geneva: World Health Organization, 1998), and from Lawrence K. Altman, "Parts of Africa Showing H.I.V. in 1 in 4 Adults," *New York Times,* 24 June 1998. AIDS as a leading cause of death in the United States from *The World Health Report 1998* and from U.S. Dept. of Health and Human Services, Centers for Disease Control and Prevention, Hyattsville, Md., *www.cdc.gov/nchswww/*, viewed January 18, 1999. Canadian AIDS rates from *AIDS in Canada: Annual Report on AIDS in Canada* (Ottawa: Health

Canada, Laboratory Centre for Disease Control [LCDC], 1996) and LCDC, "HIV and AIDS in Canada: Surveillance Report to June 30, 1998," both at *www.hc-sc.gc.ca/main/lcdc/web/publicat/aids/*, viewed January 19, 1999.

Incidence of STDs from *The World Health Report 1998*. Health impacts of STDs and 500 million couples lacking contraceptive access, from Jodi L. Jacobson, *Women's Reproductive Health: The Silent Emergency* (Washington, D.C.: Worldwatch, 1991). "One woman dies each minute" from *Population and Consumption Task Force Report* (Washington, D.C.: President's Council on Sustainable Development (PCSD), 1996). Fathalla quote from *Reproductive Health: A Key to a Brighter Future* (Geneva: World Health Organization, 1992).

Unwanted births and pregnancies from Institute of Medicine, *Best Intentions: Unintended Pregnancy and the Well-Being of Children and Families* (Washington, D.C.: National Academy Press, 1995), and from Childbirth by Choice Trust, Toronto, "Contraceptive Use in Canada," *www2.cbctrust.com/cbctrust/*, viewed June 17, 1998.

World population growth and comparison of babies' lifetime impacts (based on life expectancy and per capita GNP figures) from Population Reference Bureau, "1998 World Population Data Sheet," Washington, D.C., 1998, summary available at *www.prb.org*. Canadian and U.S. population growth based on *Statistical Abstract of the United States 1997* (Washington, D.C.: U.S. Bureau of the Census, 1997) and on Statistics Canada, Ottawa, *www.statcan.ca:80*, viewed August 3, 1998.

Share of couples using contraception from "United Nations Population Division Issues Study on Levels and Trends of Contraceptive Use As Assessed in 1994," press release, New York, 6 March 1997. Family-planning funding cuts from Alan Thein Durning and Christopher D. Crowther, *Misplaced Blame: The Real Roots of Popu-*

*lation Growth* (Seattle: Northwest Environment Watch, 1997). Lack of insurance coverage from *Population and Consumption Task Force Report* and from Peter T. Kilborn, "Pressure Growing to Cover the Cost of Birth Control," *New York Times,* 2 August 1998.

One out of five British men from "How Reliable Are Condoms?" Condoms' failure rates and proper use from Alan Guttmacher Institute, New York, "Facts in Brief: Contraceptive Use," *www.agi-usa.org/ pubs/fb_contraceptives.html,* viewed June 4, 1998. Lack of sex education and frequent U.S. contraceptive misuse from *Population and Consumption Task Force Report.* Abstinence education from Tamar Lewin, "States Slow to Take U.S. Aid to Teach Sexual Abstinence," *New York Times,* 8 May 1997.

Natural vs. synthetic rubber from Wade Davis, *One River: Explorations and Discoveries in the Amazon Rain Forest* (New York: Touchstone, 1996). Condom-tire comparisons based on weighing of Trojan condoms and packaging (twelve-pack), Kevin Jost, "Tire Materials and Construction," *Automotive Engineering,* October 1992, and on Arsen J. Darnay, ed., *Manufacturing USA,* Vol. 1 (Detroit: Gale, 1995).

Nonoxynol-9 side effects from Stephan D. Fihn et al., "Association Between Use of Spermicide-coated Condoms and *Escherichia coli* Urinary Tract Infection in Young Women," *American Journal of Epidemiology,* 1 September 1996. Frequency and costs of UTIs from Markus J. Steiner and Willard Cates, Jr., "Condoms and Urinary Tract Infections: Is Nonoxynol-9 the Problem or the Solution?" *Epidemiology,* November 1997. Endocrine effects of N-9 from A. S. Bourinbaiar, "Nonoxynol-9 as a Xenobiotic with Endocrine Activity," *AIDS,* October 1997, and from Colborn et al., *Our Stolen Future.*

THE CEILING FAN

New U.S. houses with air-conditioning and Japanese compact fluo-rescent fixtures from David Malin Roodman and Nicholas Lenssen, *A Building Revolution: How Ecology and Health Concerns Are Transforming Construction* (Washington, D.C.: Worldwatch, 1995). Canadian households with air-conditioning from Statistics Canada, Household Surveys Division, Ottawa, "Household Facilities and Equipment," Catalogue 64-202, annual, various years. Share of U.S. homes having air-conditioning, having ceiling fans, and failing to adjust thermostats from U.S. Dept. of Energy, Energy Information Administration (EIA), "Detailed Housing Characteristics Tables," in *Residential Energy Consumption Survey 1997, www.eia.doe.gov/emeu/recs/97tblhp.html,* viewed July 20, 1998.

Air-conditioning's share of U.S. electricity from EIA, *Household Energy Consumption and Expenditures, 1993,* available at *www.eia.doe.gov/emeu/recs/recs1d.html.* Air-conditioning's share of U.S. peak power load, "can set a thermostat 9°F higher," Davis tract house, lighting's share of U.S. electricity, and Lovins' quote from von Weizsäcker, Lovins, and Lovins, *Factor Four.*

Electricity-caused air pollution from Daniel Lashof, "Electricity Competition: Dirty or Clean?" U.S. Climate Action Network *Hotline,* November 1996, and from A. Jaques et al., *Trends in Canada's Greenhouse Gas Emissions 1990–1995* (Ottawa: Environment Canada, 1997). Pollution caused by average air-conditioning, "each degree you turn up the thermostat," and buildings' total energy and electricity use from Richard Heede et al., *Homemade Money: How to Save Energy and Dollars in Your Home* (Snowmass, Colo.: Rocky Mountain Institute, 1995).

Exports of HVAC from "Degree of Comfort," *Appliance,* November 1997. India from "India's Cool Competitor," *Appliance*, October 1997. CFCs from Brown et al., *Vital Signs 1998*.

Cost comparison from *Consumer Reports Buying Guide 1998* (Yonkers, N.Y.: Consumers Union, 1997). Per capita energy consumption from *Statistical Abstract of the United States 1996* (Washington, D.C.: U.S. Bureau of the Census, 1996) and from Irfan Hashmi, "Energy Consumption Among the G-7 Countries," *Canadian Economic Observer* (Statistics Canada, Ottawa), 7 May 1995.

Deregulation based on John C. Ryan, *Over Our Heads: A Local Look at Global Climate* (Seattle: Northwest Environment Watch, 1997). Taxes from Alan Thein Durning and Yoram Bauman, *Tax Shift* (Seattle: Northwest Environment Watch, 1998). Effect of casual dress from Gerald Cler et al., *Commercial Space Cooling and Air Handling: Technology Atlas* (Boulder, Colo.: E Source, 1997), abstract available at *www.esource.com*.

Floor lamp numbers; solar and CFL comparisons; and fires and universities from Lawrence Berkeley National Laboratory (LBNL), Berkeley, Cal., "Quick Facts about Halogen and Torchieres," *eande.lbl.gov/BTP/facts.html*. Nationwide halogen lamp power consumption from Marla C. Sanchez et al., "Miscellaneous Electricity Use in the U.S. Residential Sector," LBNL, April 1998. Electricity consumption in the United States from *World Resources 1998–99*.

## THE CLOTHESLINE

Dryers' electricity costs and moisture sensor energy savings from U.S. Dept. of Energy (DOE), Energy Efficiency and Renewable Energy Network, "Clothes Dryers," *www.eren.doe.gov/buildings/consumer_information/*, viewed July 17, 1998. Clothing expenditures in the United States from *Statistical Abstract of the United States 1998*.

Dryer history and watt-hours per load based on Jennifer Bennett, "On the Clothesline," *Utne Reader*, May/June 1993. Households in the United States having electric and gas dryers and those using clotheslines from DOE, Energy Information Administration, Washington, D.C., "1997 Residential Energy Consumption Survey," *www.eia.doe.gov/emeu/consumption/index.html*, viewed July 20, 1998. Historical data on dryer ownership from *Statistical Abstract of the United States* (Washington, D.C.: U.S. Bureau of the Census, annual) and from Statistics Canada, Household Surveys Division, "Household Facilities and Equipment." Clothesline bans from Richard D. Smyser, "Better to Enshrine Than to Ban the Flapping Clothesline," *The OakRidger*, 26 August 1997, available at *www.oakridger.com*, and from Bennett, "On the Clothesline."

Renewables' share of world energy from *World Resources 1996–97*. Clothesline paradox from Steve Baer, *Sunspots: An Exploration of Solar Energy through Fact and Fiction* (Albuquerque, N.M.: Zomeworks, 1979).

Six to eight loads per week from "Laundry Solutions," *Appliance*, n.d., *www.appliance.com/psarchives/ps.arch.laundry.4.htm*, viewed September 20, 1998, and from Dalhousie University Polytechnic, Canadian Residential Energy End-Use Data and Analysis Centre, Halifax, N.S., *enerInfo Residential* (newsletter), July 1996, available at *is.dal.ca/~creedac/news.html*. Dryers' share of home electricity use from Rocky Mountain Institute, Snowmass, Colo., "Home Energy Brief #6: Washers, Dryers & Misc. Appliances," available at *www.rmi.org/hebs/heb6/heb6.html*. Carbon dioxide emissions based on Heede et al., *Homemade Money*, and on A. Jaques et al., *Trends in Canada's Greenhouse Gas Emissions 1990–1995*. Three kilowatt-hours per load from Bennett, "On the Clothesline."

Microwave dryers from the Electric Power Research Institute, Palo Alto, Cal., *www.epri.com*, viewed July 23, 1998.

Solar energy reaching Earth's surface and Israeli solar hot water heaters from Christopher Flavin and Nicholas Lenssen, *Power Surge: Guide to the Coming Energy Revolution* (New York: Norton, 1994). World commercial energy production from *World Resources 1998–99*. Rooftop solar potential in the United States and European and global wind power trends from Christopher Flavin and Seth Dunn, *Rising Sun, Gathering Winds: Policies to Stabilize the Climate and Strengthen Economies* (Washington, D.C.: Worldwatch, 1997). Wind potential in the United States, wind power costs, and dropping PV costs from Douglas H. Ogden, *Boosting Prosperity: Reducing the Threat of Global Climate Change through Sustainable Energy Investments* (Washington, D.C: Environmental Information Center, 1996).

Energy costs of washers vs. dryers from Franklin Associates, "Resource and Environmental Profile Analysis of a Manufactured Apparel Product," prepared for the American Fiber Manufacturers Association, Washington, D.C., June 1993, as cited in Ryan and Durning, *Stuff*. Percentage of home energy use for hot water heating based on EIA, *Household Energy Consumption and Expenditures, 1993*, available at *www.eia.doe.gov/emeu/recs/recs1d.html*.

Passive solar design from Chris Herman, "Passive Solar in the Northwest," *EcoBuilding Times*, fall 1996. Half a million PV homes from Christopher Flavin and Molly O'Meara, "A Boom in Solar PVs," *World Watch*, September/October 1998. Sales, investment, and growth of PVs from Brown et al., *Vital Signs 1998*.

Canadian wind farms from Canadian Wind Energy Association, Calgary, "Quick Facts," *www.canwea.ca*, viewed September 10, 1998. Wind turbine noise from Stuart Baird, Energy Educators of Ontario, "Energy Fact Sheet: Wind Energy," 1993, available at International

Council for Local Environmental Initiatives, *www.iclei.org/efacts/wind.htm*. Risk to birds from Steward Lowther, "Impacts, Mitigation and Monitoring: A Summary of Current Knowledge," paper presented at *Wind Turbines and Birds* seminar, March 1996, summarized at British Wind Energy Association, London, *www.bwea.com/bird-sh.htm*, viewed September 3, 1998, and from Danish Wind Turbine Manufacturers Association, Copenhagen, "Birds and Wind Turbines," *www.windpower.dk/tour/env/birds.htm*, viewed July 23, 1998.

Japanese solar initiative from Jeremy Leggett, "Fuelling Solar Power," *ReInsurance*, March 1997, Flavin and Dunn, *Rising Sun, Gathering Winds*, and from Brown et al., *Vital Signs 1998*.

Population without electricity from Leggett, "Fuelling Solar Power." Canadian and U.S. subsidies from Flavin and Dunn, *Rising Sun, Gathering Winds*. Danish turbine sales from American Wind Energy Association, Washington, D.C., "World Wind Industry Grew by Record Amount in 1997," press release, 30 January 1998, available at *www.igc.apc.org/awea/news/news9801intl.html*.

Bonneville Power Administration from Kevin Bell, "The Unbearable Rightness of Green," *Cascadia Times*, August 1997. Student clothesline protest from Middlebury College, Office of Public Affairs, "Student Activists Have a New Line at Middlebury College," press release, Middlebury, Vt., 13 February 1997, available at *www.middlebury.edu/~pubaff/press97/clothes.html*.

## PAD THAI

Most common Thai foods and *farang* foods from Marilyn Walker, "A Survey of Food Consumption in Thailand," University of Victoria, Centre for Asia-Pacific Initiatives, Victoria, B.C., Occasional Paper, 11 June 1996.

Asian restaurant trends from Carolyn Walkup, "Asian Invasion

Sweeps U.S. As Sushi, Noodles Become Mainstream," *Nation's Restaurant News*, 15 December 1997, and from "Asian Accents," *Restaurant Hospitality*, June 1997. Supermarkets from Stephanie Thompson, "Spice of Life," *Brandweek*, 1 September 1997.

Fish consumption from *Food Balance Sheets* (Rome: Food and Agriculture Organization of the United Nations [FAO], 1996). Per capita rice consumption in the United States from *Agriculture Factbook 1997* (Washington, D.C.: USDA, Office of Communications, 1997), available at *www.usda.gov/news/pubs/*. Share as beer from USDA, Economic Research Service (ERS), Washington, D.C., "Rice Outlook, May 1998," available at *jan.mannlib.cornell.edu/reports/ erssor/field/*.

Asians' calorie intake from animal products from *Sixth World Food Survey* (Rome: FAO, 1996). Rice popularity and sayings from Mahabub Hossain, "Sustaining Food Security in Asia: Economic, Social and Political Aspects," in Pacific Basin Study Center, San Francisco, on-line forum on Sustainable Development of Rice as a Primary Food, *thecity.sfsu.edu/~sustain/welcome.html*, viewed July 2, 1998.

China Project described in T. Colin Campbell and Chen Junshi, "Diet and Chronic Degenerative Diseases: Perspectives from China," *American Journal of Clinical Nutrition*, May 1994 (supplement). United States–China diet comparisons adjusted for body weight. Beijing McDonald's from Nicholas D. Kristof, "'Billions Served' (and That Was Without China)," *New York Times*, 24 April 1992. Per capita meat consumption in various nations from USDA, Foreign Agricultural Service (FAS), Washington, D.C., on-line livestock tables, available at *ffas.usda.gov/dlp/circular/1998/98-031p/ tables/livestock.html*, Alan B. Durning and Holly B. Brough, *Taking Stock: Animal Farming and the Environment* (Washington, D.C.:

Worldwatch, 1991), and from Walker, "A Survey of Food Consumption in Thailand."

Diet-cancer links from *Food, Nutrition, and the Prevention of Cancer: A Global Perspective* (Washington, D.C.: World Cancer Research Fund and American Institute for Cancer Research, 1997). Campbell prediction from "Interview: Colin Campbell," *host.envirolink.org/mcspotlight-na/people/interviews/campbell.html,* viewed July 9, 1998.

Lack of fruits and vegetables in U.S. diet from "Feeding Frenzy," *Newsweek,* 27 May 1991. Obesity from Gary Taubes, "Obesity: How Big a Problem?" *Science,* 29 May 1998. Medical costs from Neal D. Barnard et al., "The Medical Costs Attributable to Meat Consumption," *Preventive Medicine,* November 1995.

American fat intake from "Fat Intake Continues to Drop," USDA Agricultural Research Service, press release, Washington, D.C., 16 January 1996. Red meat consumption from USDA, ERS, *Red Meat Yearbook, jan.mannlib.cornell.edu/data-sets/livestock/94006/,* viewed June 16, 1998, and from Statistics Canada, Ottawa, "Per Capita Disappearance of Meats in Canada by Kind, in Pounds, from 1920," *www.statcan.ca/cgi-bin/Cansim/cansim?matrix=001182.* Red meat consumption peak from Durning and Brough, *Taking Stock,* and from Alan B. Durning, "U.S. Poultry Consumption Overtakes Beef," *World Watch,* January/February 1988.

American Cancer Society recommendation from Jane E. Brody, "Women's Heart Risk Linked to Kinds of Fats, Not Total," *New York Times,* 20 November 1997.

Livestock's role in sustainable agriculture from *A Better Row to Hoe: The Economic, Environmental, and Social Impact of Sustainable Agriculture* (St. Paul, Minn.: Northwest Area Foundation, 1994).

Ecological toll of agriculture and livestock in North America based primarily on Alan B. Durning, "Fat of the Land," *World Watch*, May/June 1991 and on *World Resources 1998–99*. Water consumption from David Pimentel et al., "Water Resources: Agriculture, the Environment, and Society," *BioScience*, February 1997. Grain used to make a pound of meat and U.S. livestock's energy consumption from Durning and Brough, *Taking Stock*.

World livestock numbers from *Production Yearbook 1996* (Rome: United Nations, FAO, 1997). Tons of manure derived from *Statistical Abstract of the United States 1996* and from M. E. Ensminger, *Beef Cattle Science* (Danville, Ill.: Interstate Printers, 1997). "About 130 times more than humans themselves create" from Worldwatch Institute, "Meat Stampede," press release, Washington, D.C., 2 July 1998. Share of nitrogen and phosphorous from Durning, "Fat of the Land." Utah hog farm from Bob Williams, "Boss Hog's New Frontier," *Raleigh News-Observer*, 3 August 1997.

Japanese pesticides from Francesca Bray, "Rice Systems in Asia and Sustainability: An Anthropological and Historical Approach," in Pacific Basin Study Center, San Francisco, on-line forum on Sustainable Development of Rice as a Primary Food, *thecity.sfsu. edu/~sustain/welcome.html*, viewed July 2, 1998. Methane emissions from Intergovernmental Panel on Climate Change, *Climate Change 1994: Radiative Forcing of Climate Change* (Cambridge, U.K.: Cambridge University Press, 1995), and from R. Hein et al., "An Inverse Modeling Approach to Investigate the Global Methane Cycle," *Global Biogeochemical Cycles*, March 1997.

Population projections, malnutrition, and poverty from *World Resources 1998–99*. Implications of global adoption of American diet based on *Statistical Abstract of the United States 1996*; on USDA, ERS, *Red Meat Yearbook*; and on *World Resources 1996–97*.

Acreage to support U.S. and Chinese diets from David Pimentel, "The Global Population, Food, and the Environment," in L. Westra and J. Lemons, eds., *Perspectives on Ecological Integrity* (Dordrecht, The Netherlands: Kluwer Academic, 1995).

"Halved my food's impact" refers to grain and energy savings. Most popular ethnic foods from Wilbur Zelinsky, "You Are Where You Eat," *American Demographics*, July 1987. Canadians and macaroni from Joan Skogan, "An Orange Crush: Canadians Eat More Kraft Dinner Than Anyone Else in the World," *Saturday Night*, November 1996.

THE PUBLIC LIBRARY

Average U.S. library circulation and book buying, per capita library operating expenditures, and per capita book borrowing based on *American Library Directory 1996–1997* (New Providence, N.J.: R. R. Bowker, 1996). Average U.S. library book buying is a Northwest Environment Watch estimate based on above and on Barbara Hoffert, "Book Report: What Public Libraries Buy and How Much They Spend," *Library Journal*, 15 February 1998.

Canadian library circulation and per capita book borrowing based on *Bowker Annual Library and Book Trade Almanac 1997* (New Providence, N.J.: R. R. Bowker, 1997). Canadian per capita book buying based on Statistics Canada, Ottawa, data at *www. statcan.ca:80/english/Pgdb/People/Culture/arts01a.htm*, viewed September 2, 1998; data for book purchases by Canadian libraries are not available.

Environmental savings also derived from: paper shipments to book publishers from *Pulp and Paper North American Industry Fact Book* (San Francisco: Miller Freeman, 1995); U.S. book sales from *Statistical Abstract of the United States 1996;* and specific impacts of office paper from *Paper Task Force Recommendations for Purchasing and Using Environmentally Preferable Paper* (New York: Environmental Defense Fund, 1995), assuming that the average book has 10 percent recycled content.

Global paper consumption (including paperboard) from Brown et al., *Vital Signs 1998*. Information on the Berkeley Tool Lending Library is available at *www.ci.berkeley.ca.us/bpl/tool/history.html*.

Fifty-dollar savings based on book expenditures from *Statistical Abstract of the United States 1996*. Per capita library operating expenditures from *American Library Directory 1996–1997*.

Canadian funding cutbacks from "Dividends: The Value of Public Libraries in Canada," Canadian Library Association, Ottawa, *www.cla.amlibs.ca/capl/caplcovr.htm/*, viewed September 2, 1998. U.S. funding in 1990s from Evan St. Lifer, "Book Industry Study: Libraries Spend $1.8 Billion on Books," *Library Journal*, 15 September 1997. Library referenda from Richard B. Hall, "A Decade of Solid Support," *Library Journal*, 15 June 1997. Harris quotation, U.S. spending history, system "without equal," and Europe's libraries from Michael H. Harris, *History of Libraries in the Western World* (Metuchen, N.J.: Scarecrow Press, 1995).

The U.S. library funding cuts, school library statistics, and library user demographics from Tibbett L. Speer, "Libraries from A to Z," *American Demographics*, September 1995, available at *www.demographics.com*.

Adult use of libraries from U.S. Dept. of Education, National Center for Education Statistics, Washington, D.C., "Use of Public Library Services by Households in the United States: 1996," *nces01.ed.gov:80/pubs/97446.html*, viewed January 20, 1999, and from *Canadians, Public Libraries, and the Information Highway,*

Final Report (Ottawa: Ekos Research Associates, 1998), available at *www.schoolnet.ca/ln-rb/*.

Video statistics from Video Software Dealers Association, "The Home Video Industry: A White Paper on the Future of Home Video Entertainment," 1996, *www.vsda.org/whitepaper/ whitpapr.htm*, viewed July 2, 1998; it takes one sixth of a gallon of petroleum to make a standard videocassette, according to Nikki Goldbeck and David Goldbeck, *Choose to Reuse: An Encyclopedia of Services, Products, Programs, and Charitable Organizations That Foster Reuse* (Woodstock, N.Y.: Ceres Press, 1995).

Resale industry growth from National Association of Resale and Thrift Shops, St. Clair Shores, Mich., *www.narts.org*, viewed July 9, 1998, and from Carolotta G. Swarden, "Nonprofit and For-Profit Thrift Shops Battle for Customers, Merchandise," *Not for Profit Times*, May 1996, *www.nptimes.com*. Reuse trends from Kathy Stein, *Beyond Recycling: A Re-user's Guide* (Santa Fe, N.M.: Clear Light, 1997). Savings from refillables, Denmark's refills, and "90 percent of shipped goods" from Goldbeck and Goldbeck, *Choose to Reuse*. Canadian beer bottles from Teresa Coleman, Brewers' Association of Canada, Vancouver, private communication, 24 September 1998.

Containerboard waste and overnight shipping from *Preferred Packaging: Accelerating Environmental Leadership in the Overnight Shipping Industry* (Boston: The Alliance for Environmental Innovation, 1997).

THE LADYBUG

Origins of ladybug's name and larva's aphid consumption from "Lady Beetles," *Entomology Note* No. 6, Michigan Entomological Society, East Lansing, Mich., available at *insects.ummz.lsa.umich. edu/MES/notes/entnotes6.html*. Ladybug species numbers from

"Ladybird Beetle," *Columbia Encyclopedia*, Edition 5, 1993, and from Rob Simbeck, "Ladybugs," *The Conservationist*, April 1994. Adult's aphid consumption from Stephanie Bailey, "Ladybugs," Cooperative Extension Service, University of Kentucky College of Agriculture, *www.uky.edu/Agriculture/Entomology/entfacts/fldcrops/ef105.htm*, viewed April 23, 1998.

World pesticide sales from "Chemicals: Specialty" *Standard & Poor's Industry Surveys*, 23 October 1997. Value of natural pest control and volume of soil production from Robert Costanza et al., "The Value of the World's Ecosystem Services and Natural Capital," *Nature*, 15 May 1997; supplementary information posted at *www.nature.com*.

Toxicity, volume, and various problems of U.S. pesticides; delayed return of earthworms; "2 to 5 applications"; share of U.S. farmers practicing IPM; and U.S. government programs that encourage heavy pesticide use from Charles M. Benbrook et al., *Pest Management at the Crossroads* (Yonkers, N.Y.: Consumers Union, 1996).

"Flying $50 bills," reduced cotton and blueberry yields, "90 percent of world's flowering plant species," and "80 percent of world's cultivated crop species" from Mrill Ingram, Gary P. Nabhan, and Stephen Buchmann, "Ten Essential Reasons to Protect the Birds and the Bees," Forgotten Pollinators Campaign, Arizona-Sonora Desert Museum, Tuscon, Ariz., 1996, available at *www.desert.net/museum*. Quote from Stephen Buchmann and Gary Paul Nabhan, "The Pollination Crisis," *The Sciences*, July/August 1996; also see *The Forgotten Pollinators* (Washington, D.C.: Island Press, 1996). Cotton crop losses from Janet N. Abramovitz, "Valuing Nature's Services," in Lester R. Brown et al., *State of the World 1997* (New York: Norton, 1997).

Share of crops lost to pests from Edward Tenner, *Why Things*

*Bite Back: Technology and the Revenge of Unintended Consequences* (New York: Vintage, 1997), citing Robert M. May and Andrew P. Dobson, "Population Dynamics and the Rate of Evolution of Pesticide Resistance," in *Pesticide Resistance: Strategies and Tactics for Management* (Washington, D.C.: National Academy Press, 1986). Carson quote from Rachel Carson, *Silent Spring* (Boston: Houghton Mifflin, 1962).

Nations allowing DDT and tons of soil eroded per capita from *World Resources 1998–99.*

Certified organic sales in the United States from Julie Anton Dunn, "Organic Food and Fiber: An Analysis of 1994 Certified Production in the United States," USDA, Agricultural Marketing Service, Transportation and Marketing Division, Washington, D.C., September 1995. Canadian organics from George C. Myles, "Defining Moment: Canadian Organic Regs Are Coming," USDA, FAS, *www.fas.usda.gov/info/agexporter/1997/defining.html,* viewed September 29, 1998.

Farmers not seeking organic certification from *Vegetables and Specialties Situation and Outlook,* USDA, ERS, Washington, D.C., 5 May 1997, available at *http://usda.mannlib.cornell.edu/reports/erssor/.* Organic sales and acreage in the United States from Julie Anton Dunn, "Organic Foods Find Opportunity in the Natural Food Industry," *Food Review,* USDA, ERS, Washington, D.C., September–December 1995. Canadian organics from Anne Macey, past president, Canadian Organic Growers, Saltspring, B.C., private communication, April 28, 1998.

Groundwater contamination from U.S. Environmental Protection Agency, Office of Water, Washington, D.C., *National Water Quality Inventory: 1996 Report to Congress, www.epa.gov/OW/resources/9698/chap61.html,* viewed September 24, 1998.

Fertilizer discussion largely from Peter M. Vitousek et al., "Human Alteration of the Global Nitrogen Cycle: Causes and Consequences," *Issues in Ecology*, spring 1997. Half of all fertilizer ever made from "Nutrient Overload: Unbalancing the Global Nitrogen Cycle," in *World Resources 1998–99*. Recent fertilizer use trends from Brown et al., *Vital Signs 1998*.

Arizona drip irrigation from von Weizsäcker, Lovins, and Lovins, *Factor Four.* North Dakota study from *A Better Row to Hoe.*

Canadian greenhouses from Wackernagel and Rees, *Our Ecological Footprint.*

Dangers of exotic ladybugs from "Is That Ladybug Carrying a U.S. Passport?" *A&S Perspectives*, University of Washington, College of Arts and Sciences, winter 1997; "Ladybug," in Washington State University Cooperative Extension, Pullman, "Gardening in Western Washington," *www.cahe.wsu.edu/~wwmg/library/inse001/ inse001.htm*, viewed October 21, 1998, and from Daniel Simberloff and Peter Stiling, "How Risky Is Biological Control?" *Ecology*, October 1996. Store-bought ladybug dispersal from William F. Lyon, "Lady Beetle," fact sheet, Ohio State University Extension, Columbus, *www.ag.ohio-state.edu/~ohioline/hyg-fact/2000/ 2002.html*, viewed July 29, 1998. Joanna Poncavage, "Get Beneficials to Protect Your Garden!" *Organic Gardening*, May–June 1996, explains how to attract beneficial insects.

Beetle and insect species numbers from Edward O. Wilson, *The Diversity of Life* (Cambridge, Mass.: Harvard University Press, 1992). J. B. S. Haldane story from Arthur V. Evans, *An Inordinate Fondness for Beetles* (New York: Henry Holt, 1996). Wilson quote from Edward O. Wilson, "The Little Things That Run the World," *Conservation Biology*, December 1987.

## About the Author

JOHN C. RYAN is research director of Northwest Environment Watch; author of *Over Our Heads, Hazardous Handouts,* and *State of the Northwest;* and coauthor of *Stuff: The Secret Lives of Everyday Things.* He has worked for local nonprofit groups in Indonesia and for Worldwatch Institute in Washington, D.C., and holds degrees in history from Stanford and Yale Universities. John lives in Seattle, within biking distance of half a dozen Thai restaurants.

Northwest Environment Watch is an independent, not-for-profit research center based in Seattle. Its mission: to foster a sustainable economy and way of life throughout the Pacific Northwest—the biological region stretching from southern Alaska to northern California and from the Pacific Ocean to the crest of the Rockies. Northwest Environment Watch is founded on the belief that if northwesterners cannot create an environmentally sound economy in their home place—the greenest corner of history's richest civilization—then it probably cannot be done. If they can, they will set an example for the world.

To order Northwest Environment Watch books or to become a member, please call (206) 447-1880 or, toll free, (888) 643-9820. Or write to Northwest Environment Watch, 1402 Third Ave., Suite 1127, Seattle, WA 98101, USA. For more information, e-mail us at *new@northwestwatch.org,* or visit *www.northwestwatch.org.*